Museum Plantin Moretus

ANTWERP

Museum Plantin Moretus

ANTWERP

Contents

Preface

'As far as I am concerned, the criterion for a good museum is: the extent to which it is able to convey the humanity of individual people, and not so much the extent to which it represents a state, a company or a particular event'.
Orhan Pamuk.

Orhan Pamuk also put his vision of what a museum should be into practice. In his *Museum of Innocence* (Masumiyet Müzesi), he brings to life the culture of Istanbul through the lives of an imaginary couple. Emotional stories are told through meticulous compositions of everyday objects.

Emotional stories are also to be found in Christophe Plantin's home; the house of a visionary publisher, businessman, employer, printer and family man. He was the founder of a printing dynasty that continued to operate at this location through thick and thin for three hundred years. The archive and the house provide a wealth of small stories about the meaning of Christmas or laying a foundation stone, about the education of the daughters of the family and the arguments between the printers, about how the correctors, compositors and printers worked together to keep the well-oiled machine running day in, day out, about the tourists who interrupted the work and the manager who was always off on his travels... the stories are unending.

Equally unending is the wealth of printed matter produced by the *Officina Plantiniana*, with subjects ranging from religion, through linguistics, history and science, to daily life. The Officina Plantiniana formed a crossroads of knowledge, where scientists and humanists came together to have their writings printed. Plantin challenged them to continually publish new research, and distributed their books all over Europe and the colonies. He brought together the most talented people, choosing renowned authors and working only with the best type cutters, compositors, printers and illustration designers. This resulted in a list of 2500 works printed by Plantin, including some that helped influence the cultural history of Europe.

Plantin said of himself, 'I am a simple man, a printer'. Museum Plantin-Moretus tells the story of a simple immigrant who founded a family firm that formed the backbone of the dissemination of knowledge from Antwerp to every corner of the world.

Philip Heylen
Alderman for culture, the economy, urban and community maintenance, heritage and places of worship

acham. Habuit autem filios disan
hus et aran. Isti duces horreorum: dux
lotham. Dux sobal. Dux sebeon. dux
ana. dux dison. Dux eser. Dux disan.
Isti duces horreorum qui imperaverunt
in terra seyr. Reges autem qui regna
verunt in terra edom antequam habe
rent regem filii israhel. fuerunt hii.
Balech filius beor. Nomenque urbis
eius denaba. Mortuus est autem ba
lech et regnavit pro eo iobab filius
zare de bosra. Cumque mortuus esset
iobab regnavit pro eo husan de terra the
manorum. Hoc autem mortuo reg
navit pro eo adad filius badadi qui
percussit madian in regione moab.
et nomen urbis eius avith. Cumque
mortuus esset adad. regnavit pro
eo semla de masereca. Hoc quoque mor
tuo regnavit pro eo saul de fluvio ro
both. Cumque et hic obisset successit in
regnum baalan filius achobor. Isto
quoque mortuo regnavit pro eo adad.
nomenque urbis eius phou. et appella
batur uxor eius mezabel filia matred
filia mizaab. Hec ergo nomina ducum esau
in cognationibus et locis et vocabu
lis suis. Dux thamna. Dux alva.
Dux iethech. Dux oolibama. dux
ela. Dux phinon. Dux cenez. Dux
theman. Dux mabsar. Dux mag
diel. Dux hiram. Hii duces edom
habitantes in terra imperii sui. Ipse
est esau pater ydumeorum. Habi
tavit autem iacob in terra chanaan
in qua peregrinatus est pater suus
et hec sunt generationes eius.

IOseph cum sedecim esset annorum
pascebat gregem cum fratribus
suis adhuc puer et erat cum fi
liis bale et zelphe uxorum patris
sui. Accusavitque fratres suos
apud patrem crimine pessimo.
Israhel autem diligebat ioseph
super omnes filios suos eo quod in senec
tute genuisset eum. fecitque ei tunicam
polimitam. Videntes autem fratres
eius quod a patre cunctis filiis plus a
maretur oderant eum. nec poterant
ei quicquam pacificum loqui.

Accidit quoque ut visum somnium
referret fratribus suis que causa ma
ioris odii seminarium fuit. Dixit
que ad eos. Audite somnium meum
quod vidi. Putabam ligare nos
manipulos in agro et quasi consurgere
manipulum meum et stare vestros
que manipulos circumstantes adorare
manipulum meum. Responderunt
fratres eius. Numquid rex noster eris
aut subiciemur dicioni tue. Hec ergo
causa somniorum atque sermonum
invidie et odii fomitem ministravit.
Aliud quoque vidit somnium. quod
narrans fratribus ait. Vidi per som
nium quasi solem et lunam et stellas
undecim adorare me. Quod cum patri
suo et fratribus retulisset. increpavit eum
pater et dixit. Quid sibi vult hoc som
nium quod vidisti? Num ego et ma
ter tua et fratres tui adorabimus te super
terram. Invidebant igitur ei fratres
sui. pater vero rem tacitus considerabat.
Cumque fratres eius in pascendis gre

From ascetic workaholics to gentry: life in the Plantin household

Dirk Imhof

This house and the family archive tell the story of a printing dynasty. For three hundred years, the Moretus family kept the business running, through thick and thin. The extensive archive provides a wealth of anecdotes, about the birth of the children, their school results and son Balthasar living in digs in Leuven. And about their New Year wishes to one another, their travels, their grand wedding receptions and sad deaths. This is a family that rose to the nobility and displayed that rise to the world.

MON TOUT
Bien me suis lon
guement tenu
a parler des
besoignes des
lointaines
marches. Mais les prouchai
nes quant a present mont
este si fresches si nouvelles
et enclines a ma plaisan
ce que pour ce les ay mis
arriere. Mais pour tant ne
sejournoient pas les vail
lans hommes qui se desiroi
ent avancier ens ou royau
me de castille et de portingal
et aussi en gascoingne en
rouergue en quercin en li
mosin en thoulousain et en

PP. 10–11: *Wenceslas Bible*, Prague, 1403.

Jean Froissart, *Croniques*. This manuscript from the fifteenth century is a beautiful example of Flemish miniatures and describes the wars fought in Europe in the fourteenth century. Plantin probably bought the work with the idea of publishing it.

Peter Paul Rubens, *Portrait of Jeanne Rivière, Plantin's wife*.

THE NAME OF CHRISTOPHE PLANTIN and his successors, the Moretuses, lives on in the magnificent books they printed several centuries ago. However, we should not forget that besides running a successful company, they also had a life outside the printing and publishing house and bookshop. They lived in Antwerp surrounded by their colleagues, customers and friends, had children whose care made demands on their time, and family with whom they celebrated on joyful occasions or quarrelled with about money matters and inheritances. They went to school, married, travelled, fell ill and died. Thanks to the family archives preserved in the museum, a wealth of information is available about different aspects of the private lives of Plantin and the Moretuses. Space constraints meant that we had to be very selective in our choice of material, but hopefully what follows will make the reader hungry for more.

This is a story almost exclusively about members of the Moretus family, for so little is known about the personal life of Christophe Plantin. This is partly down to the paucity of surviving documentation and partly because Plantin was so absorbed in his work that Plantin the man and Plantin the businessman were pretty much one and the same person. We are completely groping in the dark when it comes to the years before he settled in Antwerp. Nothing is known for certain about his parents, his education or where he spent his early years. The exact date of his birth is also unknown (even he was unsure about it).

Something *is* known about Plantin's wife, Jeanne Rivière. She came from a village not far from Caen in Normandy where she married Plantin around 1546 while he was working for a bookseller there. Jeanne Rivière left behind no written letters or other documents. It is possible that she was illiterate. They signed Plantin's and her last will and testament with a little cross under her name. We only arrive on firmer ground in 1548 when Plantin moved to Antwerp with his wife and his eldest daughter, the two-year-old Marguerite, and registered as a citizen on 21 March 1549.

Birth and death

While information about Plantin is scanty, the same does not apply to his successor and son-in-law, Jan I Moretus. Even the time of his birth is known, because his father, Jacques Moerentorf, kept a little book of notes about the birth of his children. Next to that of his son Jan he wrote: '*Au nom de Dieu soit lan XVc et quarante trois sur ung mardy entre dilx et onze heures avant midy le xxije de may, fut ne Jan nostre secondt en lonziesme degre de aquarius au defaillant de la lune*' (In the year of the Lord 1543 on a Tuesday between 10 and 11 o'clock in the morning, on 22 May our second child Jan was born in the eleventh degree of Aquarius and as the moon was on the wane). Jan I Moretus followed the precedent set by his

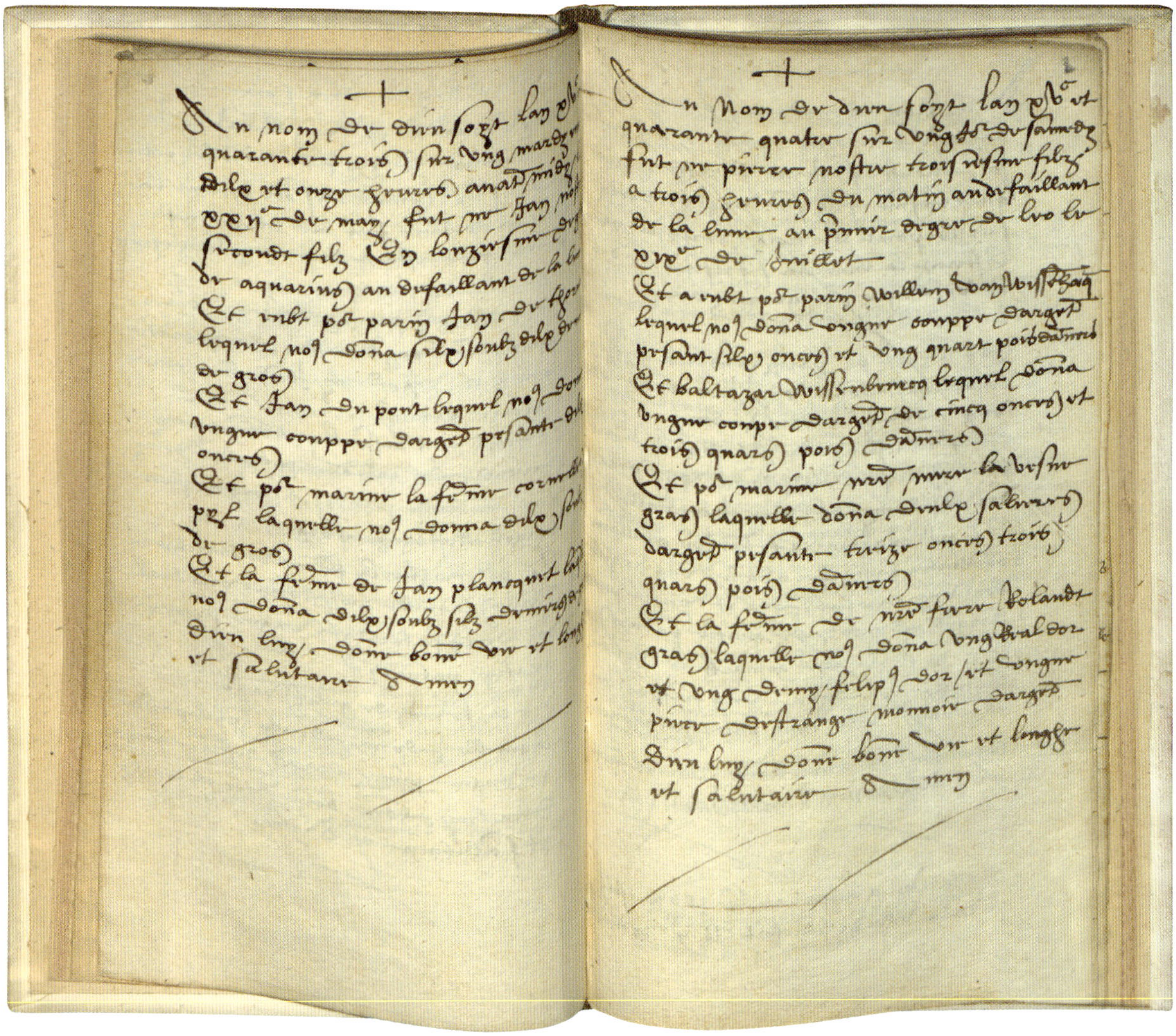

Jacques Moerentorf's note about the birth of his son Jan.

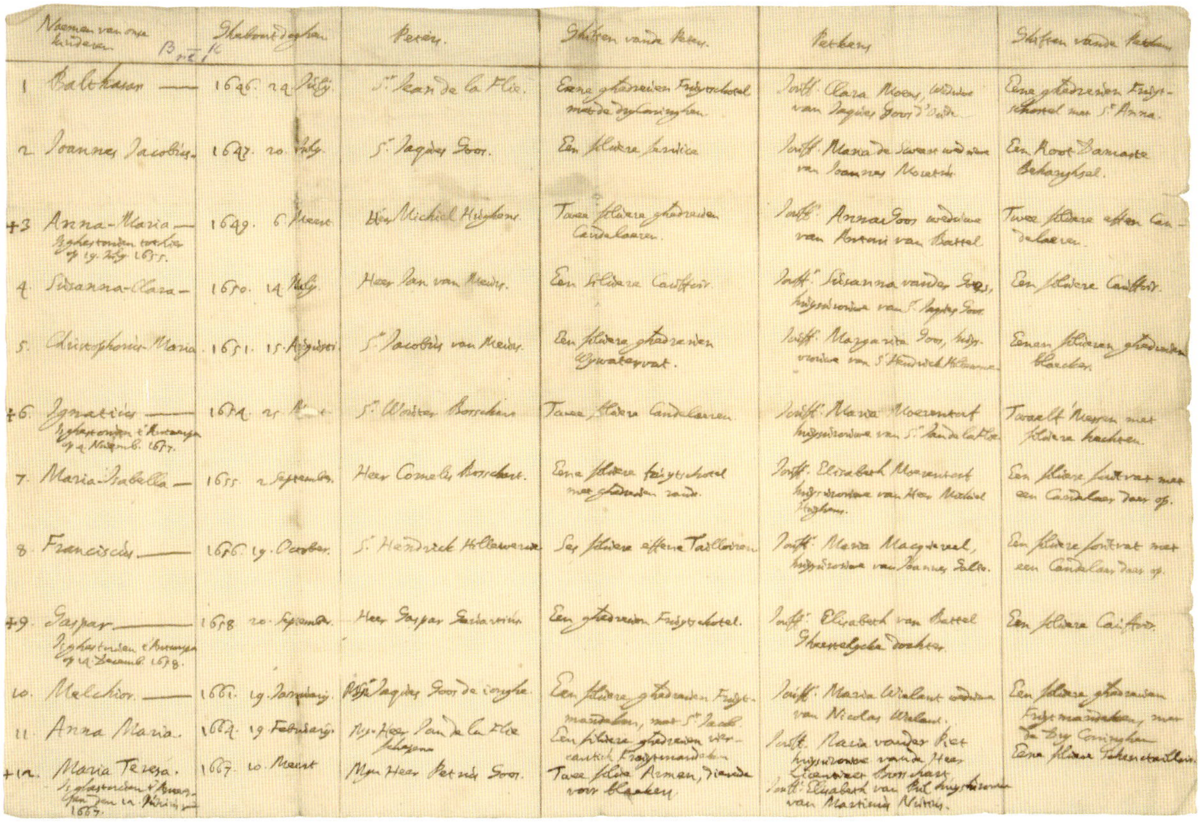

Children of Balthasar II Moretus with their godfathers and godmothers, and the gifts they received from them.

father and in his turn kept a similar book in which he recorded the most important events in his life, including the birth of his ten children. It tells us when each child was born, who the godfathers and godmothers were, but also which children died young. Only five of Jan Moretus' and Martine Plantin's children reached adulthood: Melchior, Balthasar, Jan II, Catherine and Elisabeth. The first child Gaspar died when he was twelve; the daughter Henrica who was born in 1578, died on the day she was born; another daughter, Elisabeth, who was born in 1582, died before the age of two; Adriana, born in 1586, died when she was sixteen and the last child, Christoffel, born in June 1588, did not survive more than six months.

Likewise, later members of the Moretus family often kept notes of the birthdays of their children. The grandson of Jan I Moretus, Balthasar II, drew up a table of the birth of his twelve children which included the date of birth, the names of the godfathers and godmothers and the gifts they had given to mark the birth. The list of those presents includes silver candlesticks, a silver fruit bowl, silver knives and plates, and red damask wallpaper, evidencing the increased wealth of the Moretus family. Most of Balthasar II's children who made it to adulthood, went into the church. Susanna Clara and Anna Maria became nuns, Joannes Jacobus became a Jesuit, Christophorus Maria a Minorite, Franciscus a priest at Antwerp Cathedral and Melchior a Premonstratensian. The only one not to enter the church was the eldest son, Balthasar III, who took over the Plantin publishing house after the death of his father in 1674.

In the eighteenth century Franciscus Joannes Moretus produced a veritable book of details about the birth of his children. He, too, recorded the day and time of the birth of his thirteen children and the names of their godfathers and godmothers, but he also kept a comprehensive list of the monetary gifts received from family members on each first day of the year until the child reached adulthood.

The tradition of New Year's letters dates back to the sixteenth century. Some written by several of the Moretus children have survived. As an adult Jan Moretus himself wrote several letters and poems for his father-in-law. In his turn he received letters from his children and nephews and nieces. For example, a New Year letter has survived from his nephew Karel van Tongeren dated 31 December 1602. Two sons of Joannes Jacobus Moretus kept lovely examples of a later date of New Year letters from when they had recently learned to write : there is one written by the nine-year-old Franciscus Joannes Moretus on

New Year's gifts from the family for Lodewijk Frans Moretus, the sixth child of Franciscus Joannes Moretus, from 1758 to 1767.

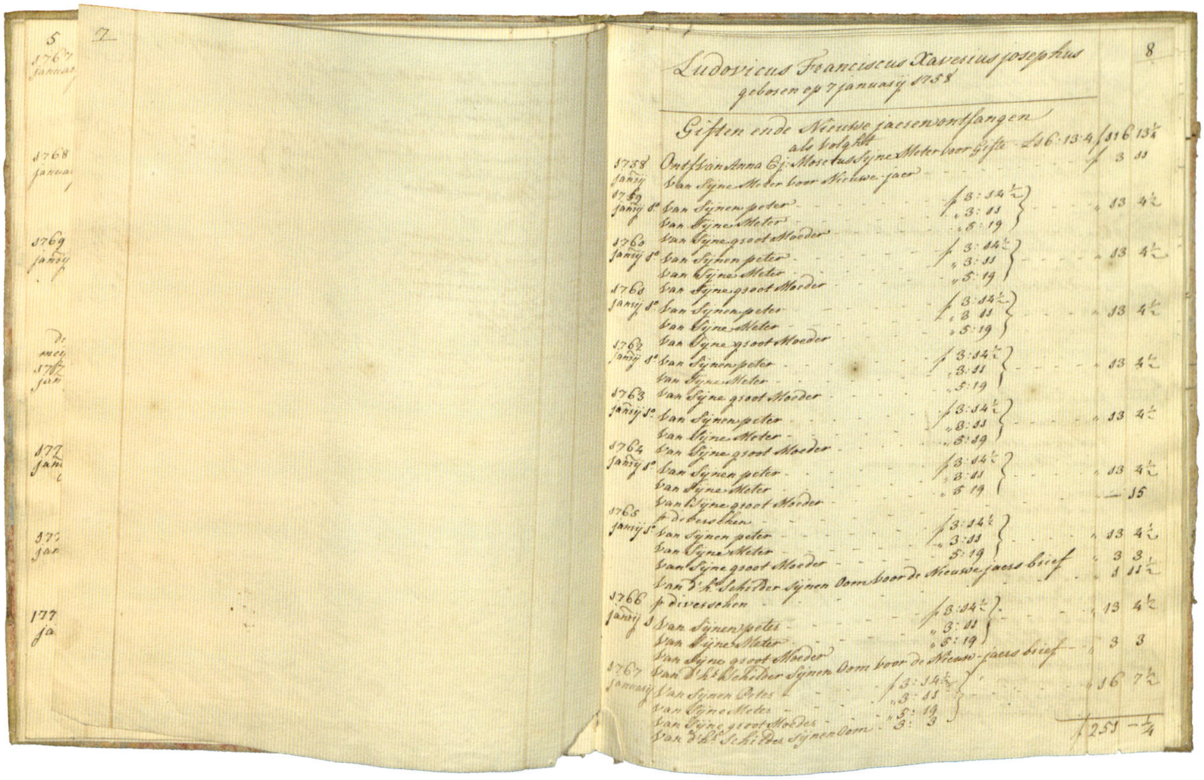
8
Ludovicus Franciscus Xaverius josephus
geboren op 7 january 1758
Giften ende Nieuwe jaeren ontfangen als volght
1758 januarij Ontf. van Anna C. J. Moretus Syne Meter voor Gifte £16:13:4 ƒ116 13¼
van Syne Meter voor Nieuwe-jaer ƒ 3 11
1759 januarij 1e van Synen peter ƒ3:14½ / van Syne Meter 3:11 / van Syne grootMoeder 5:19 — 13 4½
1760 januarij 1e van Synen peter ƒ3:14½ / van Syne Meter 3:11 / van Syne grootMoeder 5:19 — 13 4½
1761 januarij 1e van Synen peter ƒ3:14½ / van Syne Meter 3:11 / van Syne grootMoeder 5:19 — 13 4½
1762 januarij 1e van Synen peter ƒ3:14½ / van Syne Meter 3:11 / van Syne grootMoeder 5:19 — 13 4½
1763 januarij 1e van Synen peter ƒ3:14½ / van Syne Meter 3:11 / van Syne grootMoeder 5:19 — 13 4½
1764 januarij 1e van Synen peter ƒ3:14½ / van Syne Meter 3:11 / van Syne grootMoeder 5:19 — 13 4½
— 15
1765 januarij 1e van Synen peter ƒ3:14½ / van Syne Meter 3:11 / van Syne grootMoeder 5:19 — 13 4½
van d'H.r Schilder Synen Oom voor de Nieuwe-jaers brief 3 3
— 1 11½
1766 januarij 1 van Synen peter ƒ3:14½ / van Syne Meter 3:11 / van Syne grootMoeder 5:19 — 13 4½
van d'H.r Schilder Synen Oom voor de Nieuwe-jaers brief 3 3
1767 januarij van Synen Peter ƒ3:14½ / van Syne Meter 3:11 / van Syne grootMoeder 5:19 / van d'H.r Schilder Synen Oom 3:3 — 16 7½
ƒ251 — ¼

Music played an important role in the lives of well-to-do families. There are only three other examples of this extraordinary double instrument in the world. There is a harpsichord on the shorter side and a virginal a little higher up on the longer side, giving it the name of Mother and Child instrument. On the inside of the lid, a scene portraying St Cecilia is painted after Rubens.

Johannes Josephus Coenen,
Double instrument, 1734.

31 December 1726 and one written by his seven-year-old brother Paulus Jacobus on 31 December 1728.

Education

We occasionally learn something about the children's early years from family correspondence. Several letters from Martine Plantin to Jan Moretus, who represented the *Officina Plantiniana* at the book fair in Frankfurt during the early years of their marriage, passed on news (as received from the wet nurse) of the good health of their first child Gaspar.

More information is available about the education of the Plantin and Moretus children. This differed considerably from one period to another. Plantin's daughters were schooled at home. In November 1570 he wrote that he had taught his daughters to help their mother with the housekeeping and that he had also taught his four eldest daughters to read and write from the age of four or five to the age of twelve. He also allowed them to help with proofreading in the printing house and had trained them in the textile trade. Martine, his second daughter, was active in that trade from the age of thirteen and even after her engagement in 1570, at the age of twenty. After her marriage she was still fully engaged in the needlework trade until at least 1575.

When Plantin mentioned that his daughters also had to help with proofreading in his printing house this meant that the daughters could read and compare the characters in texts in different languages including Latin and Greek, but not that they understood the texts. Besides proofreading, Plantin's daughters also helped with the bookkeeping. For example, Martine kept a ledger of the weekly payments to compositors and printers from 1580 to 1590. Moreover, the eldest daughter Marguerite was given calligraphy lessons by her father. She proved to have particularly beautiful handwriting and so at the age of twelve Plantin sent her to Paris for further lessons. Problems with her eyes forced her to return home.

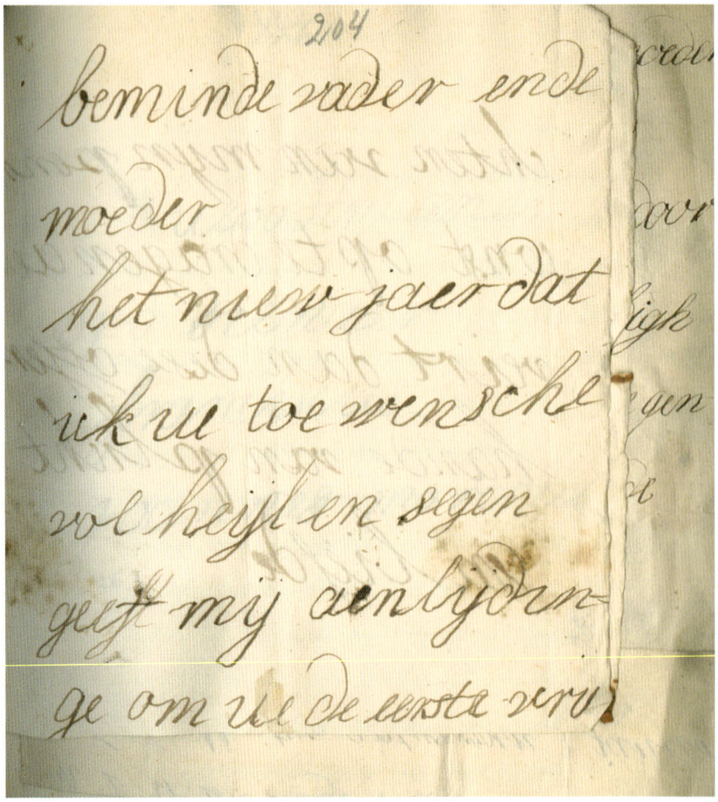
2104
bemin de vader ende
moeder
het niew jaer dat
ik ue toe wensche
vol heijl en segen
geeft mij aenlijdin
ge om ue de eerste vru

New Year's letter from Franciscus Joannes Moretus to his parents, dated 31 December 1726. 'Dear father and mother, I wish you a happy and prosperous New Year, on the occasion of which I send you the first fruits of my penmanship. Please accept this gift of duty and love'.

PP. 20–21: Caelius Sedulius, *Carmen* and Prosper of Acquitaine, *Epigrammata*, fol. 10v-11r. In the sixteenth century, this illuminated Carolingian miscellany manuscript from the ninth century came into the hands of Theodoor Poelman, who bequeathed it to Plantin.

Plantin's grandson Balthasar I Moretus lived in digs for a while with Justus Lipsius, in Parijsstraat in Leuven. His master drew up a study timetable especially for him:

6 o'clock AM: Get up, pray, wash.
Morning: Read speeches of the philosophy of Cicero for one hour. Write a letter, poem or short speech. Read Suetonius or another historian.
Afternoon: Short walk. Study Greek texts and copy out Greek sentences for one hour. Short walk. Read Homer or another poet. Read 'Letters to Atticus'. Write your own text.
After dinner: Read 'Orator ad Brutum' by Cicero, or read another author.
9 o'clock PM: Pray to God. Go to sleep.

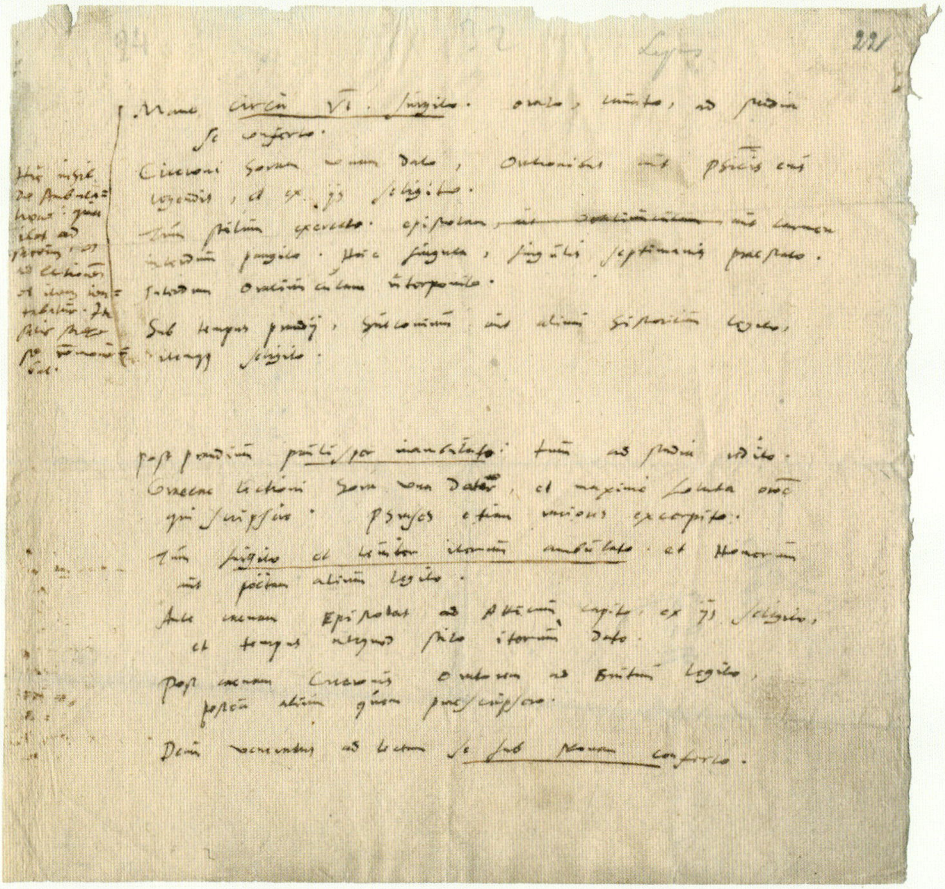

Deposuit seuisq. in faucibus iraque uenit
I ubi dicere truces predam seruare leones

Hic ubi sunt natiuitatiae post talia leges
Qui totiens tibi iurauit qui tartara iussit
Translatum nescire uirum sterilemque marito
Fecundauit anum sacram precepit ad aram
Sponte uenire pecus muliebres transtulit artus
In simulacra salis flammis incendia passos
Non ardere dedit uirgultum soluit in anguem
Perdita quis siccauit iter mirabile nimbis
Manna pluit saxo latices produxit abunde
Quadrupedem fari plano sermone coegit
Suspensis rapidas elementis distulit horas
Per uolucres hominem pauit dedit atque coruscum

ncae lum transuexit aequis iam morte grauato
fecit tria lustra uiro praedonis more
ufrago fundauit opem flagrante camino
rua uit sub rore pios per pascua regem
uit ut hirsutam pecudem tigrisq; leonum
nstimulante fame iussit uetare suis orem
empe creatori cuius quecumq; uidentur
eu quecumq; latent & rerum machina sermo est
mne suum famulatu opus sequiturq; iubentis
mperium quacumq; trahit sententia nutu
eu miseri qui fana colunt qui corde sinistro
eligio sibi sculpunt simulacra suumq;
actorem fugiunt & que fecere uerentur
uis furor est que tanta animos dementia ludit
t uolucrem turpemq; bouem toruumq; draconem
emihominemq; canem supplex homo pronus adoret
st aliud solem caecatis mentibus acti
firmant rerum esse patrem quia ante uideatur
lara serenatis infundere lumina terris
totum lustrare polum cum constet ab istis
abus instabilem rapidis discursibus ignem
fficium non esse suum qui q; ordine certo
nc oritur nunc occiduas demersus in horas
ariatur cum nocte uices nec semper ubiq; est
ec lumen fuit ille manens in origine mundi
um geminum sine sole diem noui sorbis habere
icilunae quoq; uecta ferunt quam crescere cum

Christophe Beys, the eldest son of Plantin's daughter Madeleine and Gilles Beys, born at the end of 1573 or beginning of 1574, also trained with Plantin in Antwerp. In 1587 Plantin made the thirteen- or fourteen-year-old write out his timetable in Latin as a punishment for refusing to answer when Plantin asked him to repeat the sermon of the day. He would not apologize either, but displayed a 'proud, stubborn and headstrong' attitude. The busy timetable which he had to print by way of punishment shows that he didn't have much time to himself. After school he had to read Latin proofs with his cousin Franciscus II Raphelengius.

Until the death of his father in 1558, Jan I Moretus may have attended the so-called papist school, the school of the chapter of Antwerp Cathedral, where he learned Latin. A notebook has survived in which he wrote out all kinds of Latin and Greek quotes in his last year at school. He sent his sons to the same school and also had them study music. After that his eldest son, Melchior, went to the universities of Douai and Leuven to study theology and law. Having finished papist school, his son Jan II immediately came to help in the bookshop, while Balthasar, who because of his handicap to his right arm was destined to become a proofreader, was allowed to go to Leuven for private lessons with the celebrated humanist Justus Lipsius. However, after a few months his father sent for him because he had been disobedient. He was only allowed to come and live at home after a solemn written promise of complete obedience.

Balthasar II Moretus attended the Latin schools of the Augustinians and the Jesuits in Antwerp. Then in 1630 his uncle sent him to canon Hieronymus van Winghe in Tournai where he spent two years studying and perfecting his French. In 1632, the year of his seventeenth birthday, he returned to Antwerp and from then on assisted his uncle in the company. In August 1660 at the age of fourteen, his son, Balthasar III, set off for Paris where he trained for almost three years.

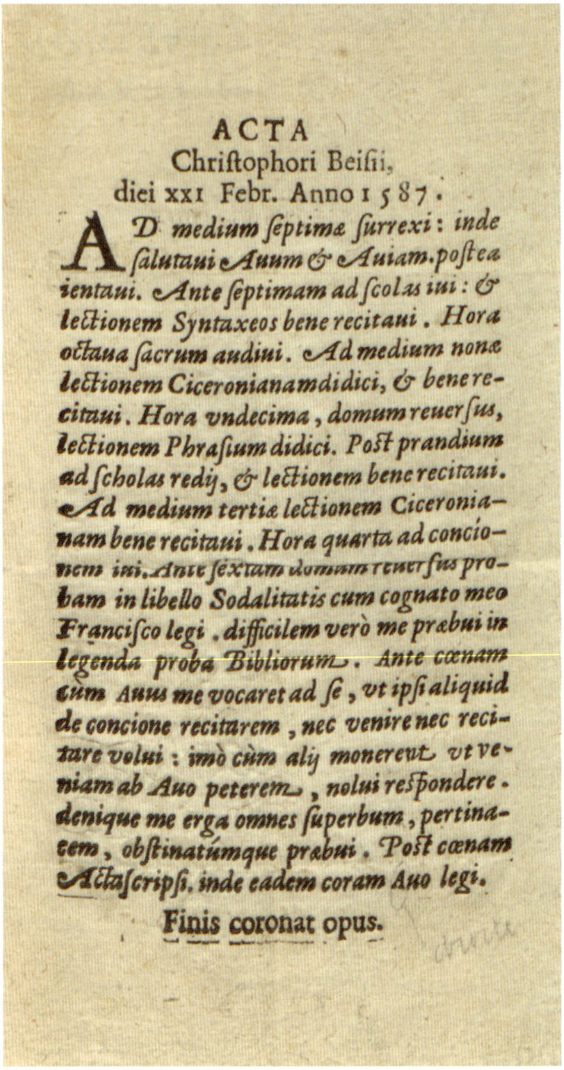
ACTA
Chriſtophori Beiſii,
diei XXI Febr. Anno 1587.

AD medium ſeptimæ ſurrexi: inde ſalutaui Auum & Auiam. poſtea ientaui. Ante ſeptimam ad ſcolas iui: & lectionem Syntaxeos bene recitaui. Hora octaua ſacrum audiui. Ad medium nonæ lectionem Ciceronianam didici, & bene recitaui. Hora vndecima, domum reuerſus, lectionem Phraſium didici. Poſt prandium ad ſcholas redij, & lectionem bene recitaui. Ad medium tertiæ lectionem Ciceronianam bene recitaui. Hora quarta ad concionem iui. Ante ſextam domum reuerſus probam in libello Sodalitatis cum cognato meo Franciſco legi. difficilem verò me præbui in legenda proba Bibliorum. Ante cœnam cum Auus me vocaret ad ſe, vt ipſi aliquid de concione recitarem, nec venire nec recitare volui: imò cùm alij monerent vt veniam ab Auo peterem, nolui reſpondere. denique me erga omnes ſuperbum, pertinacem, obſtinatúmque præbui. Poſt cœnam Acta ſcripſi. inde eadem coram Auo legi.

Finis coronat opus.

The timetable of Christophe Beys (*Acta Christophori Beisii*), 21 February 1587.

UNIVERSIS & singulis præsentes Litteras visuris pariter & audituris, PRIOR & Collegium utriusque Juris Almæ Universitatis Generalis Studii Oppidi Lovaniensis Mechliniensis Diœcesis, salutem in eo qui diligit justitiam & odit iniquitatem. Justitiæ convenit & æquitati ut quos diligenti scrutinio nostrarum Facultatum honores promeruisse comperimus eosdem ad debitos sibi gradus promoveamus, & suæ promotionis fidele testimonium non denegemus. Cùm itaque Prænobilis Dominus D. JOANNES JACOBUS MORETUS Antverpiensis, in Juris Utriusque scientia tam diligenter apud Nos laboraverit ut ad gradum Baccalaureatûs ascendere & in ea amplius Fiscatûs & Decanatûs munere summa cum laude meruerit honorari: Nos ipsi veritatis testimonium perhibentes notum facimus & attestamur per præsentes dictum Dominum JOANNEM JACOBUM MORETUS adimpleto tempore studii Juris utriusque ad hoc requisito, præcedentibus Disputationibus & Repetitionibus tam publicis quàm privatis, actibusque cæteris Scholasticis, ac tandem coram Nobis examine rigoroso per eum strenuè & laudabiliter exculto, factaque per eum coram Nobis fide de vita & Religione ipsius Catholica & præstito prius juxta Pii IV. Constitutionem juramento, secundùm formam & tenorem infrascriptum: ad nostram præsentationem Reverendo admodum Amplissimo ac Eximio Viro Domino D. HERMANNO DAMEN S. Theol. Doct. & Profess. Ordin. ac Regenti, Collegii Divæi Præsidi, nec non insignis Ecclesiæ Collegiatæ D. Petri Lovanii Canonico, & cum potestate Apostolica gradus Academicos conferendi Decano, in Choro Ecclesiæ Collegiatæ S. Petri hujus Oppidi Lovaniensis, Die 31. Januarii Anno à Nativitate Domini millesimo septingentesimo decimo-tertio juxta nostrarum Facultatum morem, statuta & consuetudines, servatis quoque solemnitatibus debitis & consuetis in Utroque Jure Licentiæ gradum honorificè suscepisse cum omnibus suis juribus, honoribus & prærogativis, etiam cum summa laude & gloria. Prædicti verò juramenti quod præstitit forma est ejusmodi: Ego JOANNES JACOBUS MORETUS firma Fide credo & profiteor omnia & singula quæ continentur in Symbolo Fidei, videlicet: *Credo in unum Deum Patrem omnipotentem, factorem Cæli & terræ, visibilium omnium & invisibilium. Et in unum Dominum JESUM CHRISTUM Filium Dei unigenitum. Et ex Patre natum ante omnia sæcula, Deum de Deo, lumen de lumine, Deum verum de Deo vero. Genitum, non factum, consubstantialem Patri, per quem omnia facta sunt. Qui propter nos homines, & propter nostram salutem descendit de Cœlis. Et incarnatus est de Spiritu Sancto ex MARIA Virgine, & homo factus est. Crucifixus etiam pro nobis sub Pontio Pilato passus & sepultus est. Et resurrexit tertia die secundùm Scripturas. Et ascendit in Cœlum, sedet ad dextram Patris. Et iterum venturus est cum gloria judicare vivos & mortuos, cujus regni non erit finis. Et in Spiritum Sanctum Dominum & vivificantem, qui ex Patre Filioque procedit. Qui cum Patre & Filio simul adoratur & conglorificatur, qui locutus est per Prophetas. Et unam Sanctam, Catholicam, & Apostolicam Ecclesiam. Confiteor unum Baptisma in remissionem peccatorum. Et exspecto resurrectionem mortuorum, & vitam venturi sæculi, Amen.* Apostolicas, & Ecclesiasticas traditiones, reliquasque ejusdem Ecclesiæ observationes & constitutiones firmissimè admitto & amplector. Item Scripturam Sacram, juxta eum sensum quem tenuit & tenet Sancta Mater Ecclesia, cujus est judicare de vero sensu & interpretatione Sacrarum Scripturarum admitto, nec eam unquam nisi juxta unanimem consensum Patrum accipiam & interpretabor. Profiteor quoque septem esse verè & propriè Sacramenta novæ Legis, à JESU CHRISTO Domino nostro instituta atque ad salutem humani generis, licet non omnia singulis necessaria; scilicet Baptismum, Confirmationem, Eucharistiam, Pœnitentiam, Extremam Unctionem, Ordinem, & Matrimonium, illaque gratiam conferre: & ex his Baptismum, Confirmationem & Ordinem sine Sacrilegio reiterari non posse. Receptos quoque & approbatos Ecclesiæ Catholicæ ritus in supradictorum omnium Sacramentorum solemni administratione recipio & admitto. Omnia & singula quæ de peccato originali & de justificatione in Sacrosancta Tridentina Synodo definita & declarata fuerunt, amplector & recipio. Profiteor pariter in Missa offerri Deo verum, proprium & propitiatorium Sacrificium pro vivis & defunctis, atque in Sanctissimo Eucharistiæ Sacramento esse verè, realiter & substantialiter Corpus & Sanguinem, una cum anima & Divinitate Domini nostri JESU CHRISTI, fierique conversionem totius substantiæ panis in Corpus, & totius substantiæ vini in Sanguinem, quam conversionem Catholica Ecclesia transubstantiationem appellat. Fateor etiam sub altera tantùm specie totum atque integrum Christum, verumque Sacramentum sumi. Constanter teneo Purgatorium esse, animasque ibi detentas fidelium suffragiis juvari, similiter & Sanctos unà cum Christo regnantes, venerandos atque invocandos esse, eosque Orationes Deo pro nobis offerre, atque eorum Reliquias esse venerandas. Firmiter assero Imagines Christi ac Deiparæ semper Virginis, nec non aliorum Sanctorum habendas & retinendas esse, atque eis debitum honorem & venerationem impertiendam. Indulgentiarum etiam potestatem à Christo in Ecclesia relictam fuisse, illarumque usum Christiano populo maximè salutarem esse affirmo. Sanctam Catholicam & Apostolicam Romanam Ecclesiam, omnium Ecclesiarum Matrem & Magistram agnosco: Romanoque Pontifici B. Petri Apostolorum Principis Successori, ac Jesu Christi Vicario veram obedientiam spondeo ac juro. Cætera item omnia à Sacris Canonibus & Oecumenicis Conciliis, ac præcipuè à sacro-sancta Tridentina Synodo tradita, definita & declarata, indubitanter recipio atque profiteor: simulque contraria omnia, atque hæreses quascumque ab Ecclesia damnatas, rejectas & anathematizatas, ego pariter damno, rejicio & anathematizo. Hanc verò Catholicam fidem, extra quam nemo salvus esse potest, quam in præsenti spontè profiteor & veraciter teneo, eandem integram & immaculatam usque ad extremum vitæ spiritum constantissimè, Deo adjuvante, retinere & profiteri, atque à meis subditis vel illis, quorum cura ad me in munere meo spectabit, teneri, doceri & prædicari, quantum in me erit curaturum. Ego idem JOANNES JACOBUS MORETUS spondeo, voveo & juro: sic me Deus adjuvet, & hæc Sancta Dei Evangelia. In cujus rei testimonium nostræ Facultatis Juris Utriusque Sigillum præsentibus Litteris duximus appendendum. Datum Lovanii Anno 1713 Mensis Januarii die 31.

Certificat de l'université de Louvain en faveur de J. J. Moretus, 8 February 1713.

Balthasar IV was the last Moretus to train in the book trade. He first attended school in Lier, before following an apprenticeship in Lille with the French printer and bookseller Francois Fievet.

From the late seventeenth century the Moretuses received a university education. Joannes Jacobus Moretus was the first director of the *Officina Plantiniana* to gain a university degree. He went to college in Douai and Leuven and became a lawyer. His successor Franciscus Joannes Moretus studied philosophy in Douai and graduated in 1742. The Moretuses no longer acquired their printing knowhow from hands-on practice, but from all kinds of notebooks. A knowledge of investments and financial transactions was now more relevant to them.

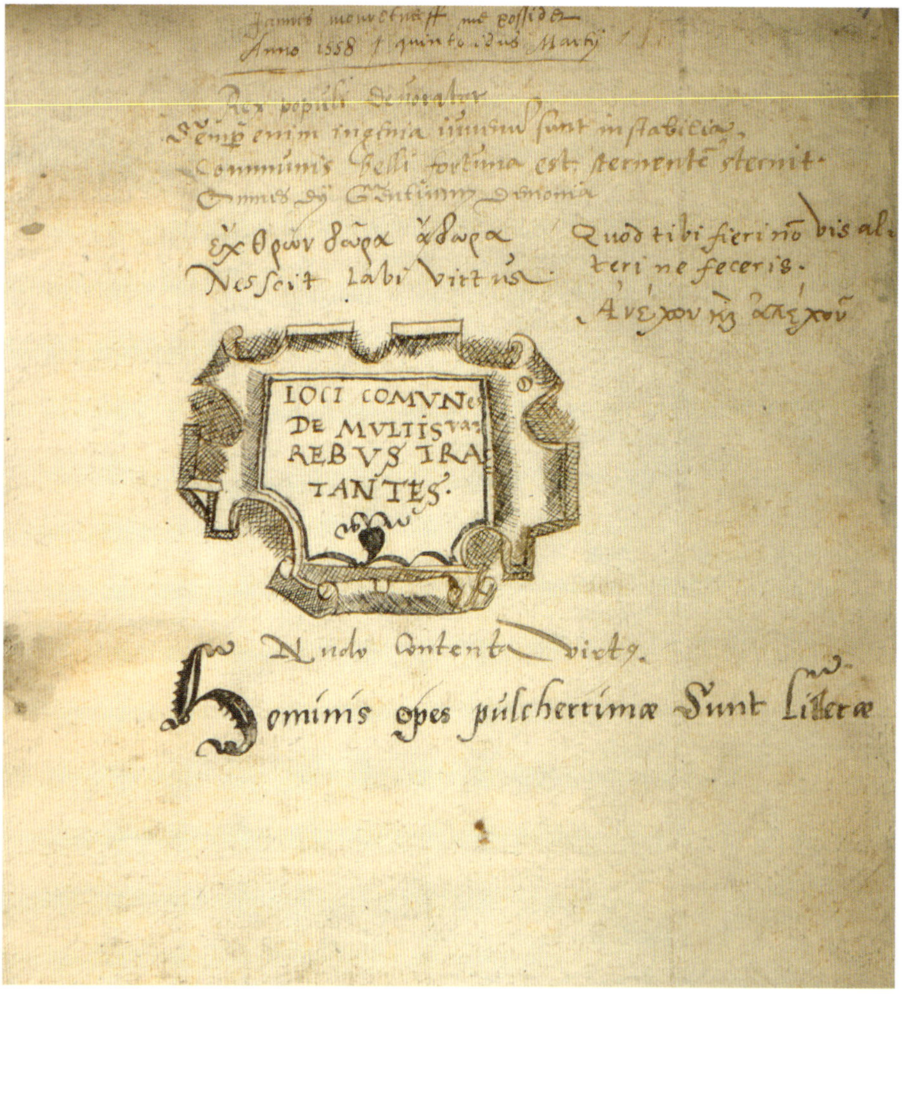

Schoolbook of Jan I Moretus: *Loci communes de multis rebus tractantes*, fol. 1r: 'Joannes Moureteuerff me possidet Anno 1558, quinto idus Martij'.

An extensive family

We know nothing at all about Plantin's family. According to the great-grandson Balthasar II Moretus, his wife Jeanne Rivière had six brothers, three of whom went into the church and three into the French army where they became captains. Apart from that one story there is no further reference to those brothers and we don't even know how reliable that statement is, for Balthasar II wrote it almost a hundred years later.

Unlike Plantin, much of Jan I Moretus' time was taken up with a whole host of problems relating to distant and close family members. In his own family his unstable son, the priest Melchior, was a source of solicitude for years, causing him many a headache and costing him a great deal of money. After his studies and ordination Melchior returned to live with his parents, but because of his mental health issues he had to be cared for elsewhere. Jan I Moretus was eventually able to find him a

Anonymous, *Tortoiseshell cabinet with 23 small paintings on white marble*, first half of the seventeenth century.
The Plantin house had numerous tortoiseshell cabinets. The two writing cabinets still kept in the museum are listed in the deed of sale from 1876. An inventory of the home of the deceased from 1691 shows that the writing cabinet in the big draw-ing room contained a small flower painting, 24 gloves, ivories, miniature portraits and fans.

room at the convent of the Bogaarden friars where he was given board and lodging for life. For years his father tried to arrange a benefice for him. In the end he had to settle for a place for him in Sint-Oedenroede near 's-Hertogenbosch.

Jan I Moretus' brothers and sisters also turned to him when they had problems. He regularly had to get his brother Michiel out of debt, as well as his brother-in-law Michel Lucart, a textile dyer in Lille, who was married to his sister Clara. Not only did he have to intervene to have Lucart released from prison, but over the years Lucart also built up a considerable debt with him. By 1592 it amounted to five hundred guilders. The wedding celebration of Lucart's daughter Marie in 1594 presented the perfect opportunity to settle the matter. Jan I Moretus chose his moment well.

On his death another distant family member, Karel de Candele, the brother-in-law of Jan's mother Adriana Gras, left two young girls who Jan Moretus took into his home until they married. Martine, Jan's wife, kept a careful record of expenditure on clothing, shoes and schooling so that once they were adults the girls would be able to repay their debt. Jan I Moretus' brother-in-law, Gillis Beys, with whom he had had heated arguments over a couple of years about the inheritance, left his youngest son in the care of Martine and Jan Moretus when he returned to Paris in 1594. The family in Paris, where Plantin's daughter Madeleine had married Jeremie Perier after Beys' death, was constantly at loggerheads. Jan Moretus and his brother Peter often had to separate the quarrelling parties. No wonder that at a certain point it all became too much for Jan Moretus and in an angry letter he ordered his son Melchior not to trouble him any longer with his little caprices.

Fortunately, the family had servants and maids to help run such a large household. Thoriken Roeckx worked as a chambermaid for Jan Moretus from 1601. She remained in service under Jan II and Balthasar I Moretus until 1628. She was allowed to stop work at the age of 84. She was not able to enjoy her retirement for long, however, for she died two years later. It has to be said that Balthasar I Moretus did pay for her burial. As help for Katelijne, the second maid, a new maid was employed, Helena van Hesen from Maaseik.

Salomon de Bray, *Portrait of Melchior Moretus.*

PP. 28–29: Gerard Mercator, *Map of the County of Flanders*, Leuven, 1540, copper engraving.

She remained in service from 1627 to 1640, the day of her engagement. The number of maids increased along with the family's status. By 1655 Balthasar II Moretus had three maids.

In addition to the domestic staff, there were also several live-in apprentices from the printing house and bookshop. So the Plantin household must have been a very busy one.

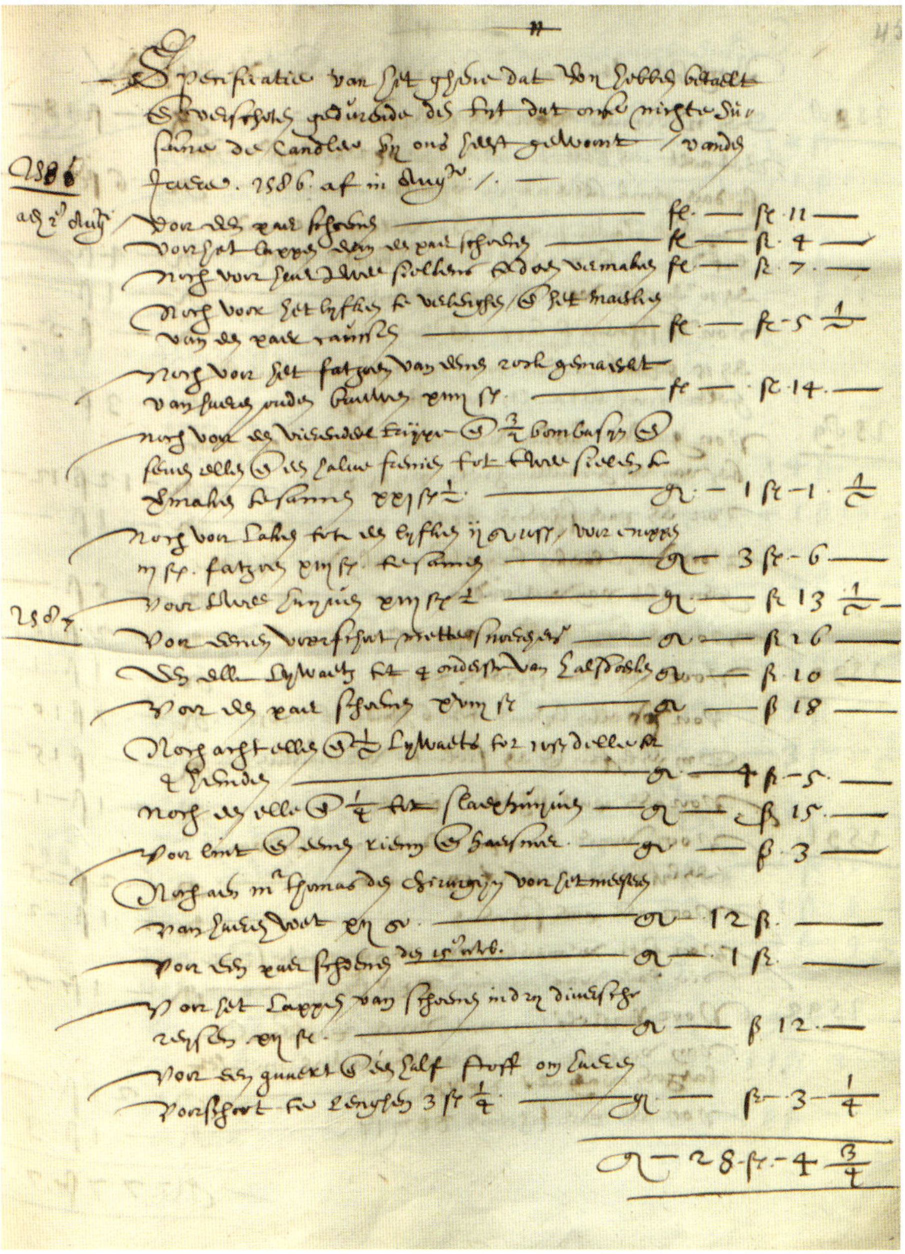

Expenses for Susanne de Candele in the years 1586 and 1587.

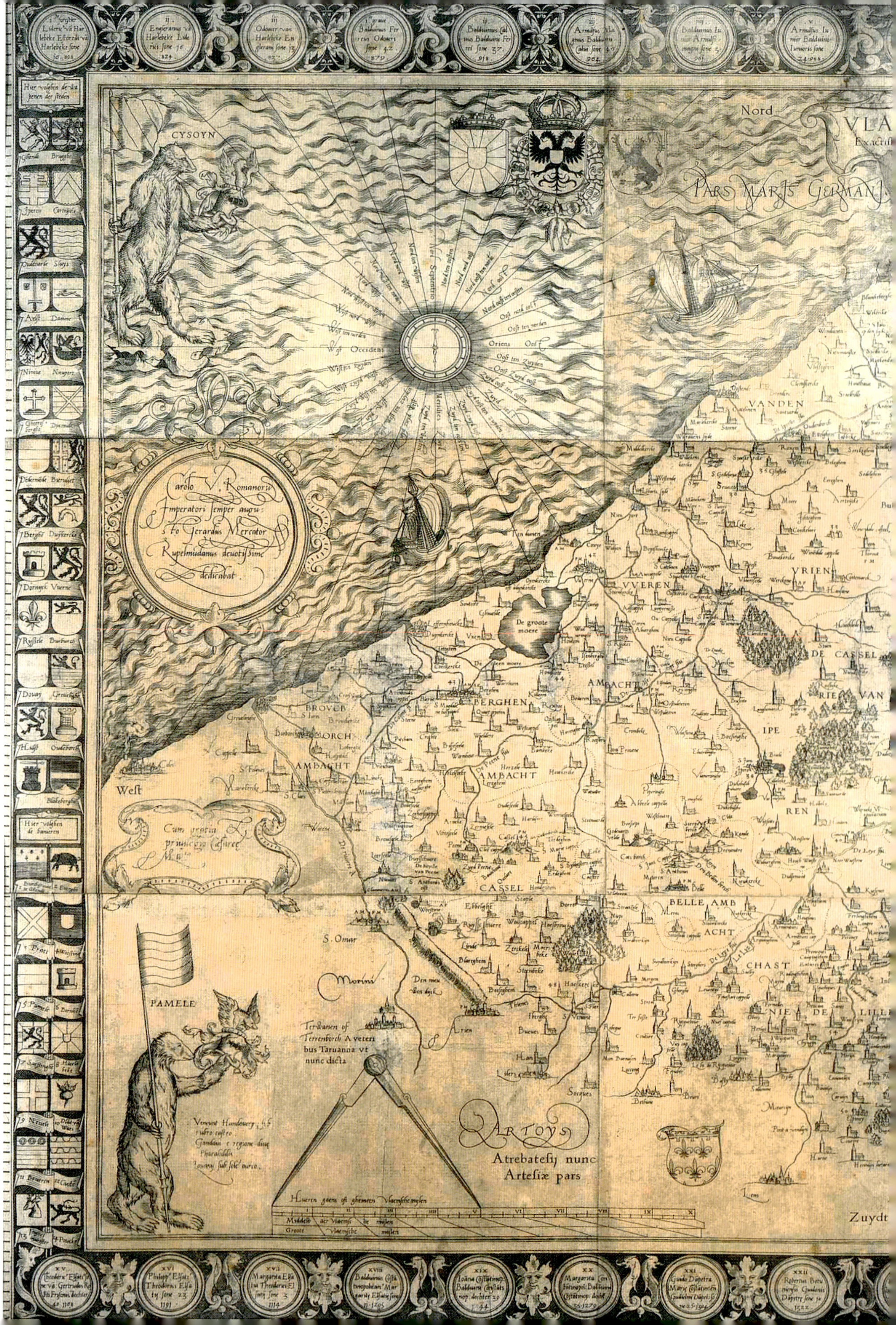
Nord
VLA
PARS MARIS GERMANI
CYSOYN
Occidens
Oriens
Carolo V. Romanoru Imperatori semper augusto Gerardus Mercator Rupelmudanus deuotissime dedicabat
De groote moere
VVEREN
VRIEN
DE CASSEL
AMBACHT
BERGHEN
IPE
REN
West
Cum gratia & priuilegio Cæsareæ Mtis
CASSEL
BELLE AMB ACHT
CHAST
S. Omar
Morini
PAMELE
Teruanen of Terrenborch A veteribus Taruanna vt nunc dicta
ARTOYS
Atrebatesij nunc Artesiæ pars
Zuydt

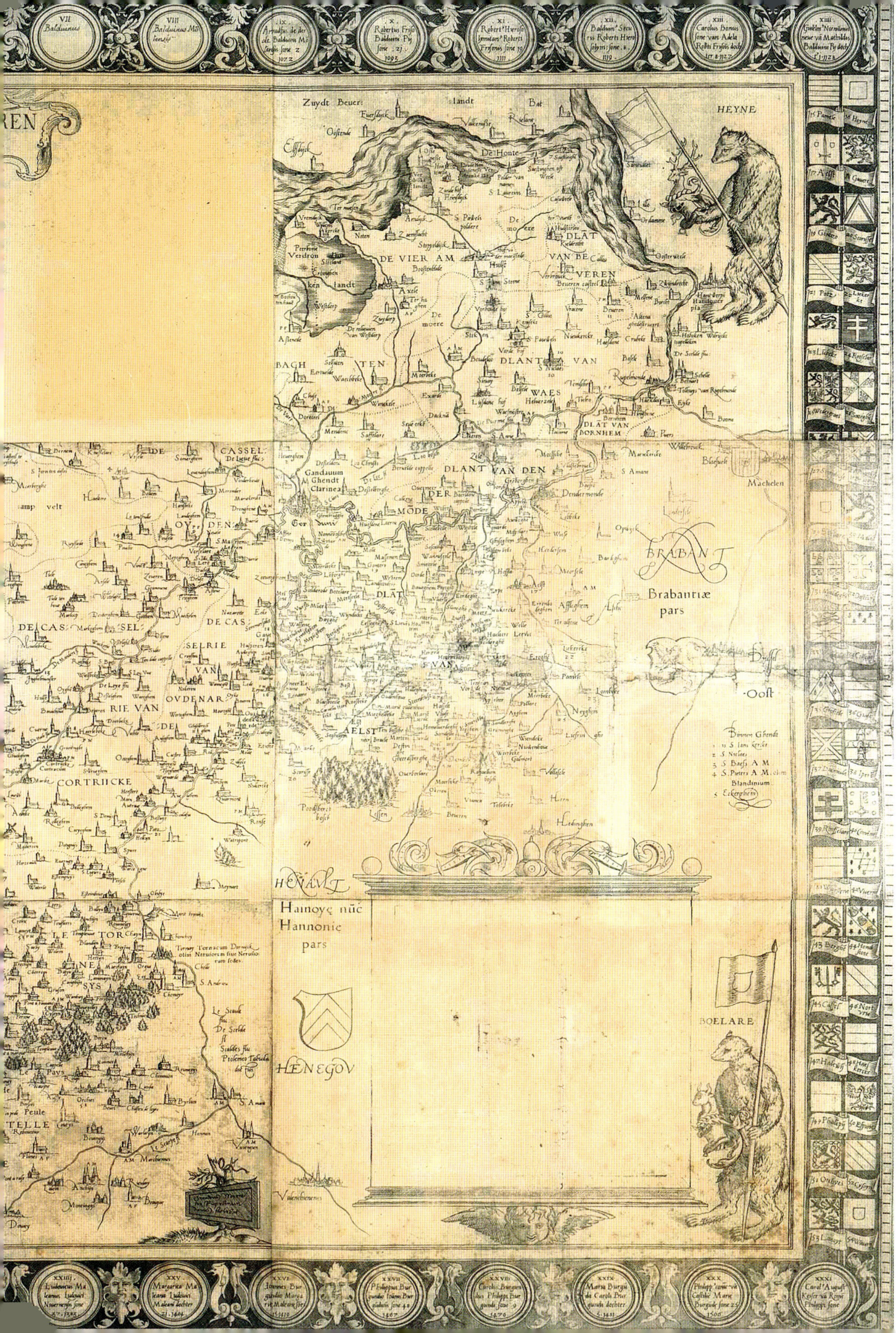

HEYNE
DE VIER AM
BACH TEN
DLANT VAN WAES
DLAT VAN BORNHEM
DLANT VAN DEN DER MODE
DLAT VAN AELST
DE CASSEL
OVDEN
DE CAS SEL
SELRIE VAN OVDENAR DE
RIE VAN CORTRICKE
LE TORNESYS
PAYS PEULE
BRABANT
Brabantiæ pars
Ooſt
HENAVLT
Hainoye nūc Hannonie pars
HENEGOV
BOELARE
Binnen Ghendt
1 S Jans kercke
2 S Niclaes
3 S Baefs A M
4 S Pieters A M
5 Eeckerghem

A life of ease

With the marriage of Jan II Moretus to Marie de Sweert in 1605 the Moretus family allied itself with a rich family of merchants from Antwerp. On 22 May 1605 the young man spoke to his bride-to-be for the first time; exactly a month later they consented to marriage and on 19 August the wedding service took place in a chapel in the cathedral. Several later family members also married young ladies from rich families and so were able to enjoy a life of ease.

Their increased wealth gave the Moretus family a taste for luxury living. Up until 1620 when Balthasar I substantially enlarged the house with an upper storey and gallery, Plantin and his sons-in-law had lived rather modestly. When he married Martina in 1570, Plantin gave Jan Moretus furniture for one room. According to Plantin, in 1575 Plantin's eldest daughter Marguerite and Franciscus I Raphelengius also lived with their three children and maid in just one room measuring 12 feet by 15 or 16 (though Plantin may have exaggerated here because he didn't want to house any more Spanish soldiers and so tried to make the situation sound worse than it actually was). Even in the 'large house' – 'grote huysinge' – which Plantin moved into on the Vrijdagmarkt in 1576, most of the space was given over to the company; paper and printed books were stored all around.

After the death of Jeanne Rivière in 1596, Jan Moretus, who until then had lived with his family above the shop in Kammenstraat, came to live in the large house known as the De Gulden Passer or The Golden Compass on the Vrijdagmarkt. It continued to be the home of every director of the Plantin printing and publishing house until the nineteenth century. Balthasar I Moretus collected artworks to furnish his enlarged 'residence'. From Peter Paul Rubens he bought portraits of family members and of leading scholars. He housed his numerous books, including all the important publications by church fathers and classical authors and works about sciences and history,

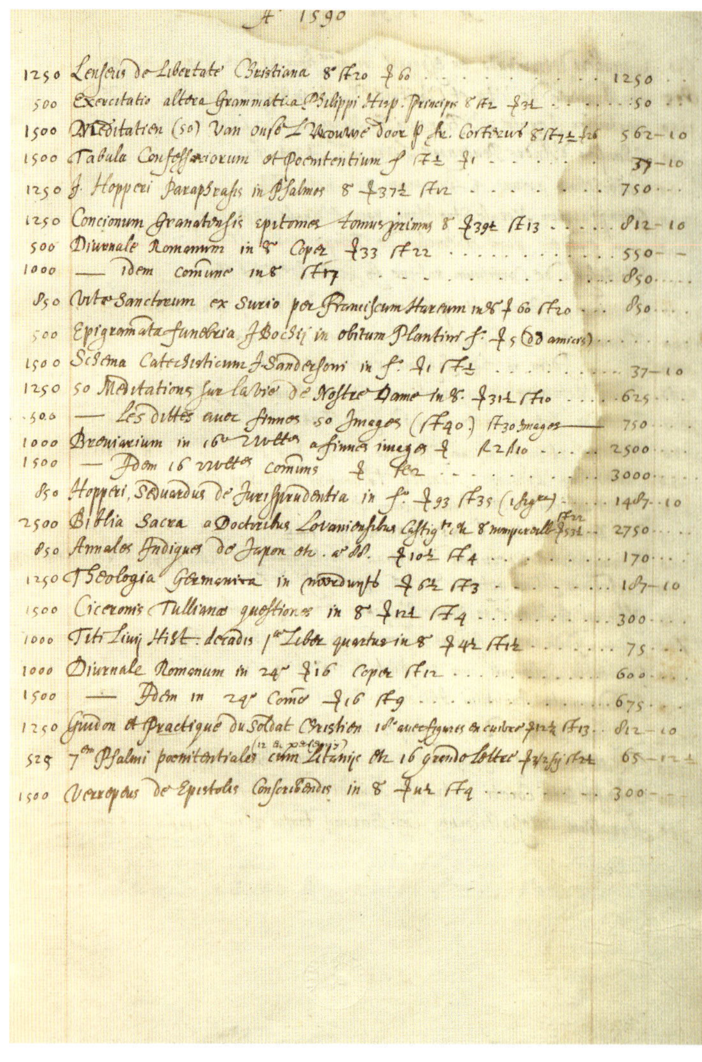

Catalogue of the private library of the Moretuses, c. 1675, first page of works on theology in folio.

Peter Paul Rubens,
Portrait of Christophe Plantin, 1613–1661,
oil on panel.

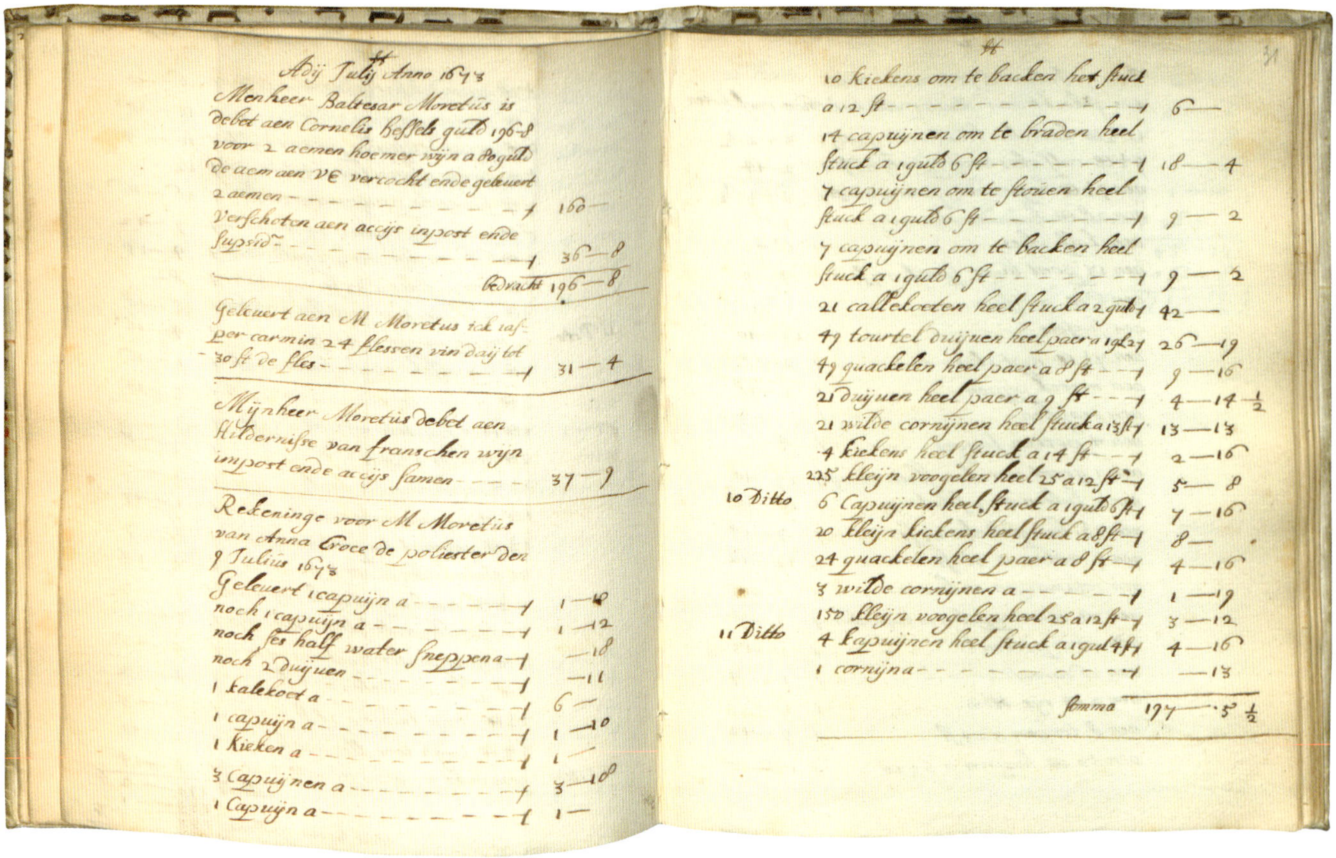

in a private library of which a catalogue compiled in 1675 listed almost 3,000 titles. Apart from paintings and books he also furnished the house with tapestries, gold leather, sculptures and costly furniture. The later Moretuses, whose wealth was even greater, systematically added to this art collection. The surviving inventories provide insight into the family possessions. The profusion of silverware, porcelain and jewellery, in addition to the numerous unusual objects, from muskets and pistols to scientific instruments and billiard tables, is staggering.

This increased affluence was displayed to their friends and acquaintances at large parties. Balthasar I Moretus kept things relatively sober, but he did like good meals and above all wine from the Rhineland. He and his sister-in-law Marie were always pleased to receive a cask of wine and Westphalian ham from acquaintances in Cologne. The later Moretuses threw caution to the winds. Festivities to mark weddings, professions or elections as head of an association were celebrated with an abundance of food and drink. The Moretuses kept a careful record of the cost of all

Deliveries for the meal for the wedding of Balthasar III Moretus and Anna Maria de Neuf on 9 July 1673.

these parties, though the quantities of oysters, hams, roast turkeys, partridges, larks and desserts of marzipan, waffles and almond biscuit were such that it could not have been easy to keep a tally. In the case of major celebrations like the marriage of Balthasar III and Anna Maria de Neuf in July 1673, it took several days to consume all the food.

Whereas Plantin and his first successors gave all their time to the company, from the second half of the seventeenth century the Moretuses found themselves with more and more free time and the opportunity to travel. In diaries they noted down which places they had visited and what the highlights had been. When Balthasar III left for Paris for three years in 1660, his father accompanied him on the outward journey. Not only did they visit the most important Parisian booksellers and libraries, but they also gazed in admiration at the Louvre, the palaces of Cardinal Richelieu and of Cardinal Mazarin, and abbeys and numerous country estates in the area.

Besides strong male entrepreneurs, a business like the Officina Plantiniana also needed women with a marked sense of entrepreneurship. Anna Goos (1627–1691) married Balthasar II Moretus, who was her elder by twelve years. Following the death of her husband in 1673, she took over the management of the *Officina Plantiniana* and led the business through a period of financial crisis, whilst also diligently managing the household. Most probably, she remained a strong support to her son when he took over the business in 1681. This portrait shows a self-confident woman dressed in the fashion of her day in expensive lace. The pearls were a wedding gift from her husband, and she inherited the brooch from her mother.

Jacob van Reesbroeck, *Anna Goos*, 1659.

After returning from Paris, in 1665 Balthasar III was given the chance to travel to Italy. Most of his descriptions of the numerous churches and monuments which his father had instructed him to visit sound dull and dutiful. Only when he writes about his visits to a stable in Naples with hundreds of mounts belonging to the king or to the carnival with dancing, Spanish music and traditional costumes do we sense his enthusiasm. Even as an adult Balthasar III Moretus still had a taste for luxury and horses. In 1680 when the Spanish monks threatened to withdraw the profitable orders for liturgical editions, Balthasar III went off to Madrid to negotiate the contract with them. During the discussions the monks offered him a small palace in the vicinity of Madrid if he would move his printing house to Spain. Balthasar III could see himself as lord and master of a Spanish

Jacob van Reesbroeck, *Portrait of Balthasar III Moretus at the age of fourteen.*

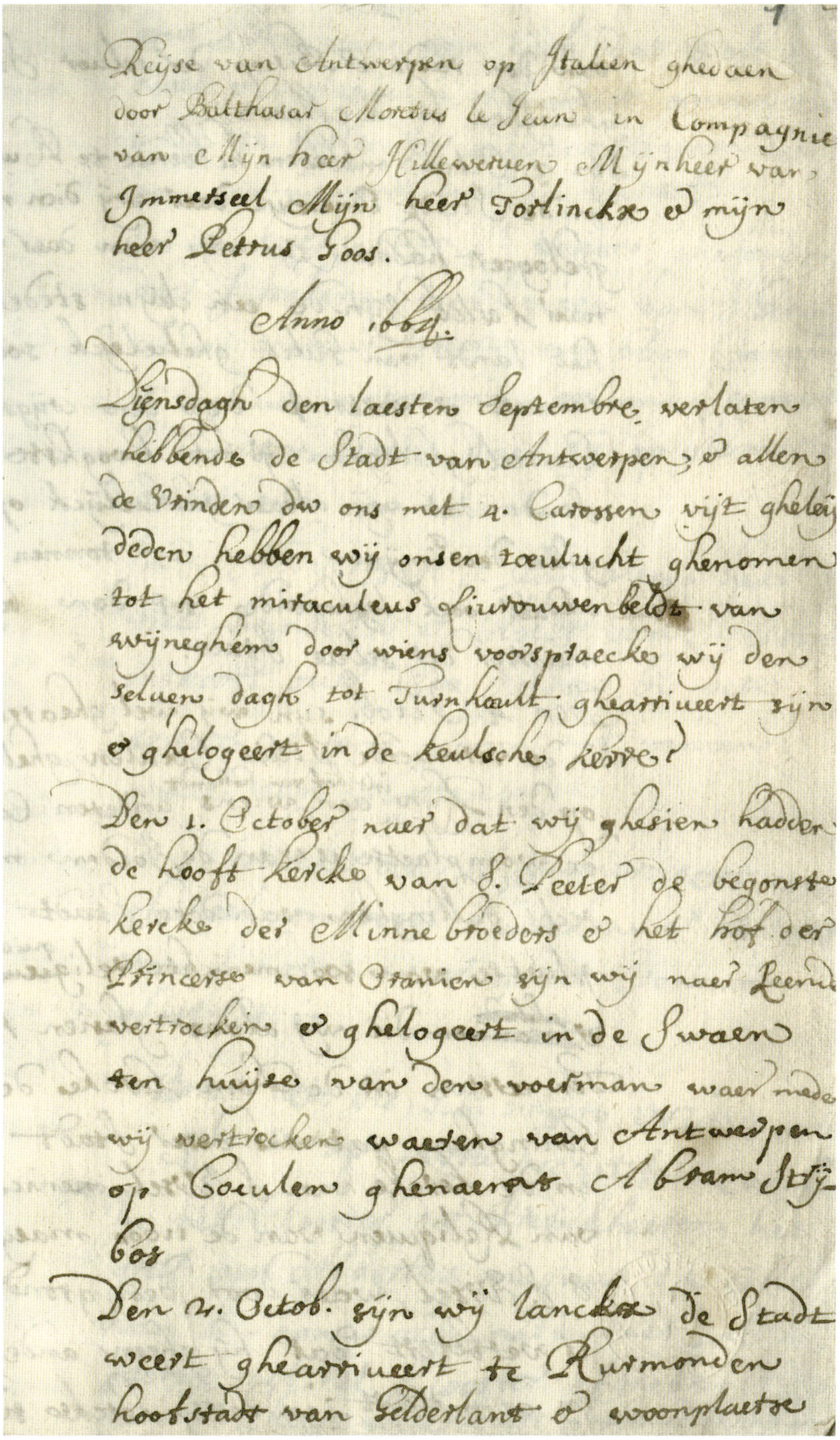
Reijse van Antwerpen op Italien ghedaen
door Balthasar Moretus le Jeun in Compagnie
van Mijn heer Hillewerven Mijnheer van
Immerseel Mijn heer Tortinckx & mijn
heer Petrus Goos.

Anno .1664.

Diensdagh den laesten Septembre verlaten
hebbende de Stadt van Antwerpen, & allen
de Vrinden die ons met 4. Carossen vijt gheleij
deden hebben wij onsen toevlucht ghenomen
tot het miraculeus Lievrouwenbeldt van
Wijneghem door wiens voorspraecke wij den
seluen dagh tot Turnhoult ghearriueert sijn
& ghelogeert in de keulsche kerre
Den 1. October naer dat wij ghesien hadden
de hooft kercke van S. Peeter de begonste
kercke der Minnebroeders & het hof der
Princesse van Oranien sijn wij naer Leende
vertrocken & ghelogeert in de Swaen
ten huijse van den voerman waer mede
wij vertrocken waeren van Antwerpen
op Coeulen ghenaempt Abram Stij-
bos
Den 2. Octob. sijn wij lanckx de Stadt
weert ghearriueert te Rurmonden
hoofstadt van Gelderlant & woonplaetse

Balthasar II Moretus, *Reijse van Antwerpen op Italien ghedaen door Balthasar Moretus le jeun* (Journey from Antwerp to Italy, undertaken by Balthasar Moretus the Younger).

castle with stables full of fine steeds and wrote an enthusiastic letter to his mother saying that he wanted to accept the offer. His mother soon brought her son back down to earth and categorically refused to consider the suggestion. Fortunately the monks did not make the move a condition of the deal and the company remained in Antwerp for us to enjoy to this day.

The fortune of several successive owners of the *Officina Plantiniana* is clear evidence of the Moretuses' increasing wealth. In 1658 Balthasar II Moretus had approximately 400,000 guilders. In 1714 Balthasar III's widow left behind 760,000 guilders. Unlike other rich families who were content to lead a life of leisure in the first half of the eighteenth century, the Moretuses continued to play an active role in the book trade. Thanks to the lucrative trade with Spain, Joannes Jacobus saw a further increase in the family fortune and when he died he left more than 1,600,000 guilders. At the end of the eighteenth century the profitable export of books to Spain came to an end, but their investments at home and abroad were such that the Moretus family's standing was unaffected.

Peter Paul Rubens, *Dying Seneca*, 1613–1616.

Arnoldus Florentinus a Langren before 1560–1642/48, *Terrestial and celestial globe*, second half of the seventeenth century. Besides books, prints and lace, Plantin also sold scientific instruments and globes. Globes were generally sold in pairs for decorating an art room or library. These globes were bought by the museum. Not only was the Langren family a dynasty of globe-makers, but they were also the best in the Southern Netherlands.

Virgilius Bononiensis, *City map of Antwerp in aerial view*, printed by Gillis I Coppens van Diest, 1565.

PIA
SCALDIS FLV
ANTVERPIA

Aristocracy

Given their wealth and growing social status, Balthasar III hoped for an aristocratic title. Several years before his death, in 1692, the coveted title of 'jonker' or 'squire' was bestowed upon him, along with special permission to continue to play an active role in the company despite his noble title. From the end of the sixteenth century the Moretuses had imagined that they were of noble birth.

Jan Moretus' mother, Adriana Gras, was the daughter of an Antwerp merchant Peter Gras. When Moretus' nephew, the priest Peter Gras, was in Milan, he heard of an aristocratic Milanese family called Grassi. He presumed that there must be a connection between the Gras and Grassi families. This similarity of names was all it took to fuel the fantasy. When Melchior Moretus gained his lawyer's degree in 1597, he had his thesis printed by the

Thesis by Melchior Moretus with the coat-of-arms of the Grassi family from Italy, Leuven, 1597.

The *Officina Plantiniana* received regular visits from writers, scholars or just tourists. But occasionally there were special visitors like kings, princes and regents. On such an occasion, the manager of the business would often receive a gift, such as a gold chain and portrait medallion. Family tradition has it that the German tower clock was a gift to Balthasar I Moretus from Archduke Albrecht and Archduchess Isabella no less.

Tower-shaped table clock, Germany (?), first quarter of the seventeenth century.

IVSTITIA · TEMPERANTIA

D. O. M.

EXIMIA VIRTVTE ET DOCTRINA CONSPICVO DOMINO, D. MELCHIORI MORETO, I. V. LAVREAM ADIPISCENTI GRATVLATVR, C. H. Q.

Pauperiore fluant, quamuis mihi carmina, vena
Tentandũ tamẽ eſt aliquid, modo Phœbus Alumnũ
Laude ſuum ornanti vires roburq́ue miniſtret.
Nam benè moratum MORETVM tollere in aſtra
Laudibus eſt animus, nomenq́ue æquare canendo
Sedibus Æthereis: coluit parnaſſia montis
Culmina, dum denos vix ipſe impleuerat annos:
Vix dubiam ſignabat humum puerilibus annis
Cum colere inſignes incepit Apollinis artes:
Has autem iuris ſtudio fœliciter auxit,
Quo meritam ecce refert magna cum laude coronam:
Namque coronatum lauro excipit, ecce virorum
Doctorumq́ue manus (ô gloria) cingit euntem.
Quiſquis MORETI ora videt, videt ora dianæ.
Nam veluti rutilum germanæ lumen opacæ,
Sol tenebroſa ſuis accendens omnia flammis
Præbet, vt ipſa nigræ pallentem Delia noctis
Horrorem excutiat, poſitu radiata benigno,
Auertatq́; nefas & quidquid iniqua virorum
Attentare manus gaudet, tunc orbe repellat
Dum ſol Oceano viduas commendat habenas.
Non aliter Deus ingenium doteſq́ue quibuſdam
Partitur datq́ue illuſtrem ad moderamina mentem.
Cum virtus olim, veluti fax ſplendida, noſtram
Illuſtrans mentem, vitijs exacta fuiſſet,
Tunc cæcos homines ſe præcipitare videres
In ſcelus omne, nouas lętantes nectere clades
Cladibus, inſanáque hominum incrudeſcere cæde.
Sed ſol iuſtitiæ diuino lumine quoſdam
Illuſtrat, trutina pendentes omnia iuſta
Et quibus, indignum tenui inſultare clienti
Cunctáque criminibus violari iura, videtur:
Quos inter ſacrum morem MORETE reducens
Cæleſti ſplendore micas, inſignia portans
Doctrinæ & cinctus viridanti tempora lauro
Carpe gradus igitur (portu ſiſtêre petito)
Doctrinaq́ue tuos ſuperis ſpectabilis illa
Qua ſplendes ſanctoq́; illuſtra lumine ciues.

LOVANII, XXVI. NOVEMB. ANNO CIↃ. IↃ. XCVII.

Apud Ioannem Maſium, ſub Viridi Cruce. 1597.

Leuven printer Jan Maes and added the coat of arms of the Grassi family as a sign of his noble birth. It was at that point that blue blood became part of the family legend. In 1606 Balthasar I Moretus claimed that the humble Plantin had belonged to an aristocratic family before he came to Antwerp, but that the family fortune and the feudal benefice had gone to his elder brother.

Up until the seventeenth century the Moretuses had avoided public office as far as possible because the company took up all their time. On several occasions they had requested exemption from positions in the city council or guild. Only exceptionally did they take on a position of responsibility. For example, Jan Moretus was 'wijkmeester' or 'district supervisor' of the sixth district of Antwerp from 1598 to 1603 in which capacity he carried out a number of administrative tasks including the collection of some taxes. As a noble family the Moretuses could no longer refuse public office. In 1685 Balthasar III Moretus became head almoner. Later Moretuses also held the post of almoner and consequently were involved in poor relief and charitable institutions such as the Berg van Barmhartigheid. They also took on responsibilities in the city council: Joannes Jacobus was alderman of Antwerp from 1727 to 1730, his son Paulus Jacobus in 1752.

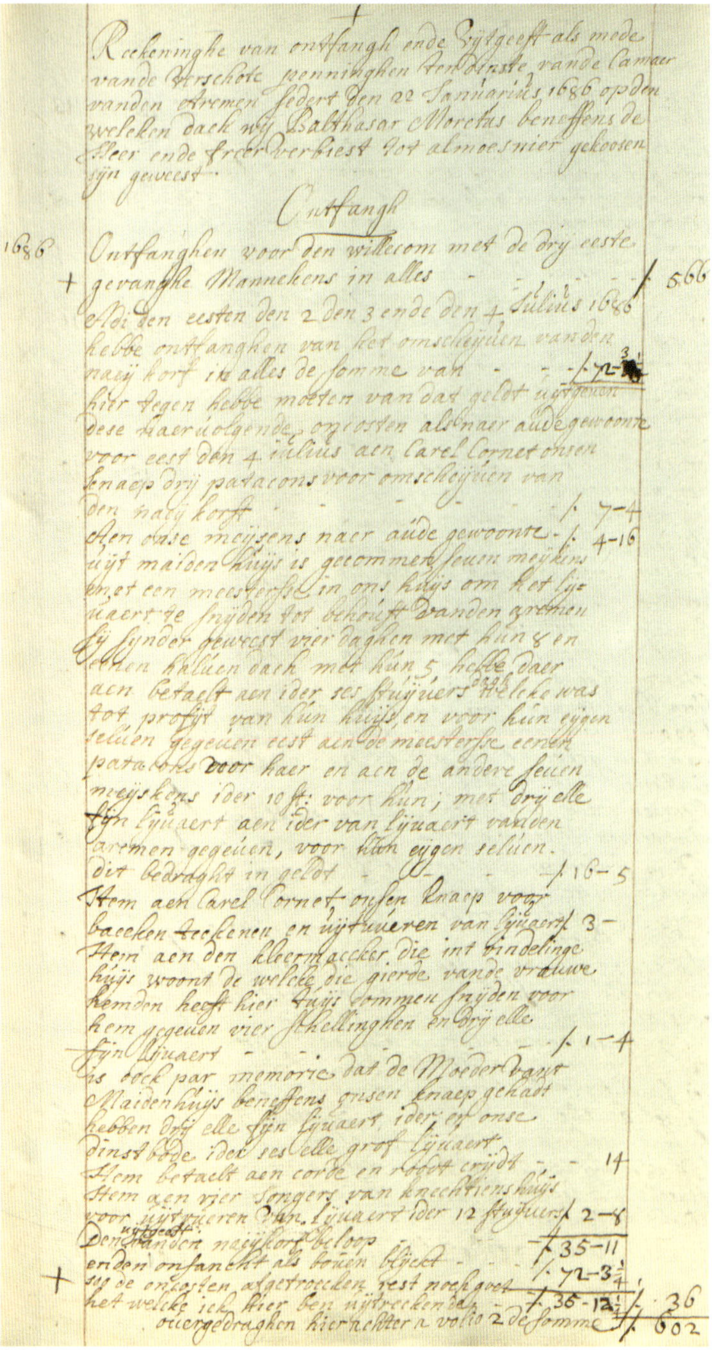

Bookkeeping done by Balthasar III as almoner in 1686.

Wealthy citizens like the Moretus family displayed their affluence by hanging expensive tapestries on the walls. At the height of the Renaissance, tapestries depicting stories from Greek mythology were very popular. They often have a moralistic message. Tomyris, queen of the Massagetae, defended her people against the Persian king Cyrus and killed him. It is a lesson in bravery and courage. The Moretus family bought these Brussels tapestries from their first owners, the Losson-van Hove family. The Moretus family crest and the Plantin compass have been worked into the borders, which were added later, in the seventeenth century. The tapestries were also cut to size, so they would fit into this drawing room.

The first drawing room with Brussels tapestries of the *Story of Tomyris and Cyrus.*

Justus Lipsius is explaining a text to two of his pupils. On his left, we see Jan Woverius, and on his right Filips Rubens, the painter's brother, who is looking over Lipsius' shoulder with interest. The four men were good friends of Balthasar I Moretus. Set in a niche is a bust of Seneca and a vase of tulips. A draped opening gives a view of the Palatine Hill in Rome. In the foreground is one of Lipsius' faithful dogs (Saphyrus?). The painting is an anonymous copy of a work by Rubens in the Palazzo Pitti in Florence.

Copy after Peter Paul Rubens, *The Four Philosophers*, seventeenth century.

Funereal roll of Sr Jan Moretus I (22 September 1610).

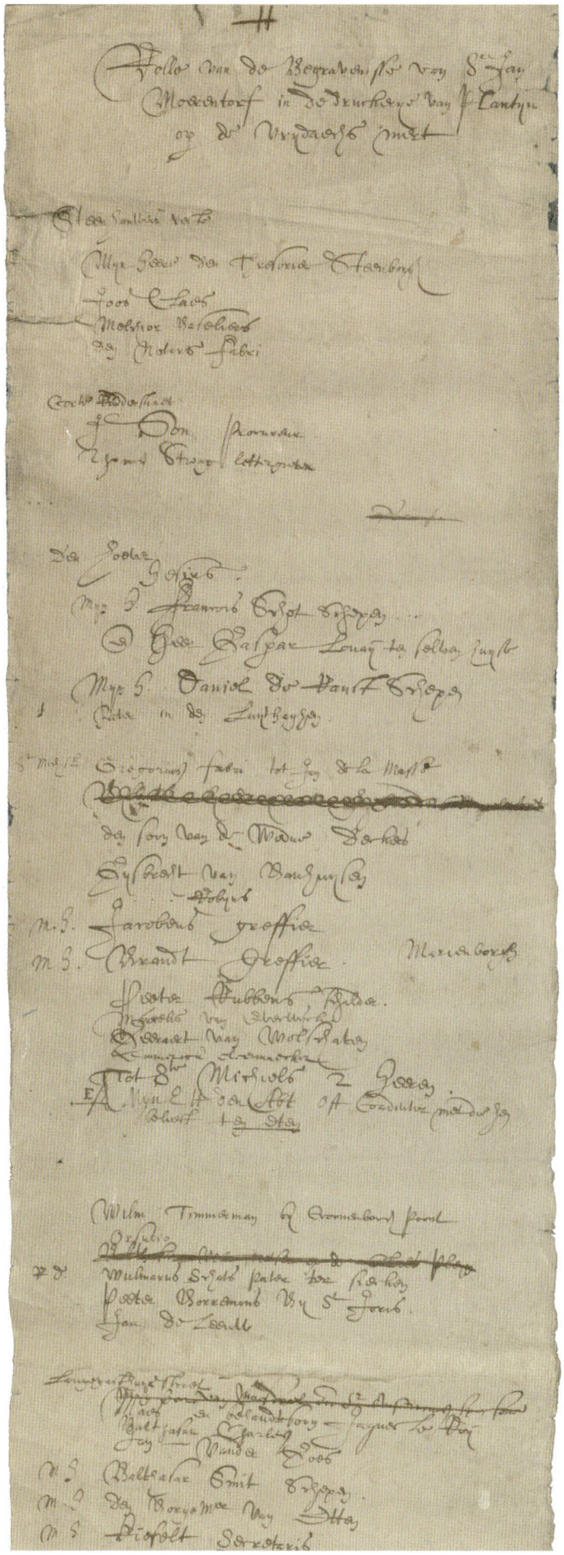

Illness and death

Rich people get sick and die too. Illness can strike at any time and prove fateful. In a letter written in October 1638 to his nephew Franciscus II Raphelengius, Balthasar I Moretus asked about a fever which had been raging in Antwerp for several months and had cost the life of his two nephews Louis and Christophe Moretus (two sons of Henrica Plantin and Peter Moretus). The death of Louis Moretus hit him particularly hard because he had worked with him for so long in the bookshop. Another employee Philips Collaert, who lived with him, had lain in bed in peril of death for fifteen days. The bookseller Martinus Nutius, who was related by marriage, had just died, too, leaving behind his very young children.

As in all aspects of their lives, the Moretuses kept a careful record of doctors' and apothecaries' bills, along with the countless purgative drinks and laxative powders they bought. His garden in Berchem was where Balthasar II Moretus liked to recover from an illness. In October 1661, he wrote, '*ben ick ghevallen in eene swaere siekte door de welcke tot in mey 1662 mijne camer hebbe moete behouden ende daer naer hebbe in de maanden junio en julio op mynen hof tot Berchem Spa water ghedroncken, waer door wederom myne volcomme gesontheyt becomen hebbe*' (fell seriously ill and had to keep to my room until May 1662, in the months of June and July drinking Spa water in my garden in Berchem, where I was restored to full health). Some ten years later, in the spring of 1671, he was again very ill with the black bile which confined him to bed for several months, but by dint of drinking Spa water for six weeks in his garden in Berchem by the summer he was his old self again. This land, on which there was also a house, was located on what is today Kardinaal Mercierlei and Grote Steenweg in Berchem. So delighted was Balthasar II with his garden that he measured its distance from several places in the city: from the Sint-Jorispoort the garden was 2,200 steps and from there to his house on the Vrijdagmarkt it was 1,500 steps, as he himself had measured on 28 February 1659. It seems he enjoyed a good walk.

Funerals were no simple matter for a rich family like the Moretuses. Not only did the various inheritances have to be settled, but there was all administrative work entailed in the bequests and memorial services. Costs for the funeral itself included the musicians during the mass, the making of mourning clothes, the painting of the funeral escutcheon and payments to coachmen, church wardens and others. There were bequests not only for distant family members, but also for company employees, domestic servants and above all for the city's many monastic orders and for the distribution of alms of various descriptions. The Moretuses wrote down the names of the guests at the funeral and the street where they lived on narrow strips of paper which were stuck to each other and were many meters long. Thanks to these lists we know where the Antwerp artists, merchants and publishers lived at the time.

All these documents which the Moretus generations preserved provide a colourful insight into numerous aspects of their lives. The sheer volume of letters, wills, inventories of their possessions and other documents bring to life the dynasty that headed up the large Plantin publishing house from the hard-working Christophe Plantin who skilfully piloted his company through the dangerous religious wars of the sixteenth century to squire Albert Moretus who tried in vain to inject new life into the old printing house in the nineteenth century. They make the books which rolled off their presses even more fascinating and worthy of our admiration and appreciation.

Costs of the illness, funeral and mourning clothes of Balthasar I Moretus.

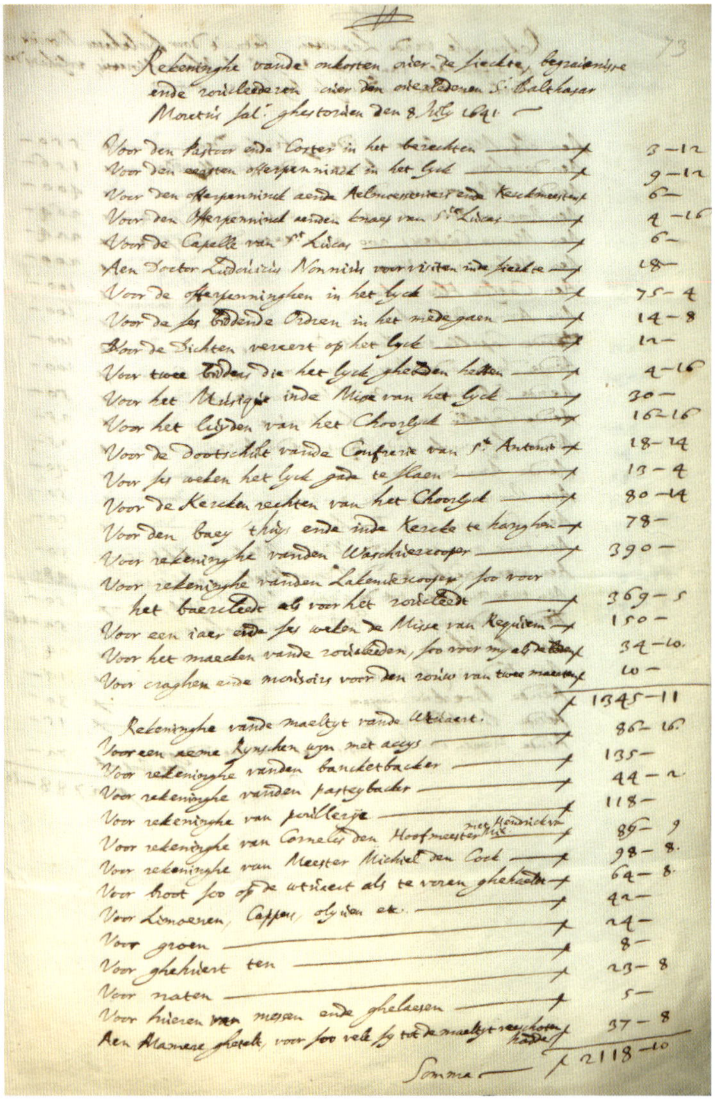

Rekeninghe vande onkosten over de sieckte, begraeffenisse ende rouwcleederen over den overleden S. Balthasar Moretus sal. ghestorven den 8 July 1641

Voor den Pastoor ende Coster in het berechten	3-12
Voor den eersten offerpenninck in het lyck	9-12
Voor den offerpenninck aende Aelmoesseniers ende Kerckmeesters	6-
Voor den offerpenninck aenden knaep van St Lucas	4-16
Voor de Capelle van St Lucas	6-
Aen Doctor Ludovicus Nonnius voor visiten inde sieckte	18-
Voor de offerpenninghen in het lyck	75-4
Voor de ses biddende Orden in het medegaen	14-8
Voor de dichten verceert op het lyck	12-
Voor twee bodens die het lyck ghebeden hebben	4-16
Voor het Musique inde Misse van het lyck	30-
Voor het luyden van het Choorlyck	16-16
Voor de dootschult vande Confrerie van St Antonis	18-14
Voor ses weken het lyck gade te slaen	13-4
Voor de Kercken rechten van het Choorlyck	80-14
Voor den baey thuys ende inde Kercke te hanghen	78-
Voor rekeninghe vanden Waschkeerscooper	390-
Voor rekeninghe vanden Lakenkooper soo voor het baercleedt als voor het rouwcleedt	369-5
Voor een iaer ende ses weken de Misse van Requiem	150-
Voor het maecken vande rouwcleeden, soo voor my als de [illegible]	34-10
Voor craghen ende [illegible] voor den rouw van twee maenden	10-
	1345-11
Rekeninghe vande maeltyt vande [illegible]	86-16
Voor een aeme Rynschen wyn met accys	135-
Voor rekeninghe vanden banketbacker	44-2
Voor rekeninghe vanden pasteybacker	118-
Voor rekeninghe van [illegible]	86-9
Voor rekeninghe van Cornelis den Hoofmeester met Hendricken	98-8
Voor rekeninghe van Meester Michiel den Cock	64-8
Voor broot soo op de uitvaert als te voren ghehaelt	42-
Voor Limoenen, Cappers, olyven etc.	24-
Voor groen	8-
Voor ghehuert ten	23-8
Voor naten	5-
Voor hieren van messen ende ghelaesen	37-8
Aen Marnese ghelt, voor soo vele sy tot de maeltyt verschoten hadde	
Somma	2118-10

Peter Paul Rubens, *The Ethiopian king Balthasar*, seventeenth century. The family once possessed a great many paintings by Rubens: the family portraits, an *Adoration of the Magi*, *The Lion Hunt* (a good copy after Rubens), portraits of Seneca and Plato, and a series of five panels depicting the Virgin Mary, Joseph and the three kings. The painting of the Moorish or Ethiopian king was sold in the eighteenth century, but bought back by the city of Antwerp in 2000.

PP. 48–49: Detail of the 'homestead of Moretus' on what is now Kardinaal Mercierlei, in Berchem, on: Pieter II Verbiest, *Map of the margraveship Antwerp*, 1662 ('Ager Antverpiensis sive pars Marchionatus sacri Romani imperii').

AGER ANTVERPIENSIS SIVE PARS MARCHIONATVS SACRI ROMANI IMP
De Heerlycheyt van Deusel acker of s Schooten
De Heer lyc heyt van Deuren en B
Burgerhout
De Bemden van
De Heer lycheyt
Merxcem
van
Merxcem
Den Polder van Merx cem
Stuyvenberg
ANTWERPE
Steenburger Waert
Den Polder van Aus
DE SCHELDE
Het Zwyn
Den Dam
Cruyningen
Deuren
Nobilissimis Am
D. IOAN. ANTO
D. ÆGIDIO M
CONSV
Reliquisq. Vrbis ANT
Thesaurariis et Q
Syndicis, Graphia
Hanc Emporij celeberrimi
Pagorum Suburbanorum accu
Petrus Verbiest sculptor Antv
Anno
Nomber 1. is het Concept vant Laer
De Meyerey vanden Bos
t'Lant van Luyck
t'Quartier van Antwerpen
De Baroni van Bredael
t'Quartier van Loven
t'Quartier Brussel
van Brussel
Vlaenderen
Bergen op Zoom
Hollant

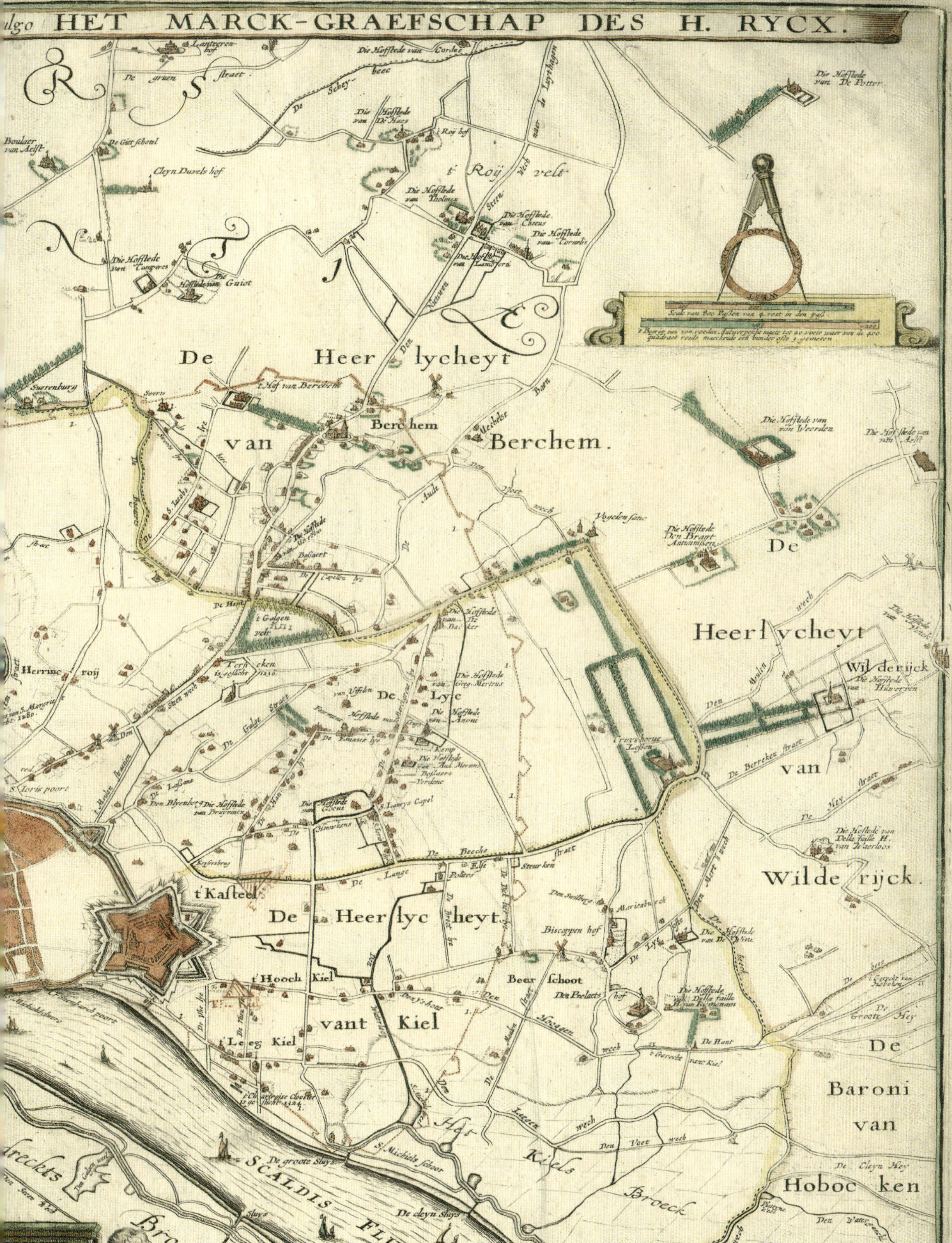

HET MARCK-GRAEFSCHAP DES H. RYCX.
De Heerlycheyt van Berchem.
Berchem
De Heerlycheyt van Wilderijck.
Wilderijck
De Lye
t'Kasteel
De Heerlycheyt vant Kiel
t'Hooch Kiel
Leeg Kiel
Bisschops hof
Beerschoot
De Baroni van Hoboc ken
Het Hobocse Broeck
Het Kiels Broeck
SCALDIS FLUVIUS
De groote Sluys
De cleyn Sluys
Burgerwaert
't Hooy schoor
Suerenburg
Herrinc roij
t'Roij velt
De Kiebse Sluys
De Broeck Sluys
Broeck
Tot Antwerpen Gedruckt by Peeter Verbiest.

1 בְּרֵאשִׁית בָּרָא אֱלֹהִים אֵת הַשָּׁמַיִם וְאֵת
2 הָאָרֶץ׃ וְהָאָרֶץ הָיְתָה תֹהוּ וָבֹהוּ וְחֹשֶׁךְ
עַל־פְּנֵי תְהוֹם וְרוּחַ אֱלֹהִים מְרַחֶפֶת עַל־
3 פְּנֵי הַמָּיִם׃ וַיֹּאמֶר אֱלֹהִים יְהִי־אוֹר
4 וַיְהִי־אוֹר׃ וַיַּרְא אֱלֹהִים אֶת־הָאוֹר כִּי־טוֹב וַיַּבְדֵּל
5 אֱלֹהִים בֵּין הָאוֹר וּבֵין הַחֹשֶׁךְ׃ וַיִּקְרָא אֱלֹהִים לָאוֹר
יוֹם וְלַחֹשֶׁךְ קָרָא לָיְלָה וַיְהִי־עֶרֶב וַיְהִי־בֹקֶר יוֹם אֶחָד׃
6 וַיֹּאמֶר אֱלֹהִים יְהִי רָקִיעַ בְּתוֹךְ הַמָּיִם וִיהִי מַבְדִּיל
7 בֵּין מַיִם לָמָיִם׃ וַיַּעַשׂ אֱלֹהִים אֶת־הָרָקִיעַ וַיַּבְדֵּל בֵּין
הַמַּיִם אֲשֶׁר מִתַּחַת לָרָקִיעַ וּבֵין הַמַּיִם אֲשֶׁר מֵעַל לָרָקִיעַ
8 וַיְהִי־כֵן׃ וַיִּקְרָא אֱלֹהִים לָרָקִיעַ שָׁמָיִם וַיְהִי־עֶרֶב
9 וַיְהִי־בֹקֶר יוֹם שֵׁנִי׃ וַיֹּאמֶר אֱלֹהִים יִקָּווּ הַמַּיִם
מִתַּחַת הַשָּׁמַיִם אֶל־מָקוֹם אֶחָד וְתֵרָאֶה הַיַּבָּשָׁה וַיְהִי־
10 כֵן׃ וַיִּקְרָא אֱלֹהִים לַיַּבָּשָׁה אֶרֶץ וּלְמִקְוֵה הַמַּיִם קָרָא
11 יַמִּים וַיַּרְא אֱלֹהִים כִּי־טוֹב׃ וַיֹּאמֶר אֱלֹהִים תַּדְשֵׁא
הָאָרֶץ דֶּשֶׁא עֵשֶׂב מַזְרִיעַ זֶרַע עֵץ פְּרִי עֹשֶׂה פְּרִי לְמִינוֹ
12 אֲשֶׁר זַרְעוֹ־בוֹ עַל־הָאָרֶץ וַיְהִי־כֵן׃ וַתּוֹצֵא הָאָרֶץ דֶּשֶׁא
עֵשֶׂב מַזְרִיעַ זֶרַע לְמִינֵהוּ וְעֵץ עֹשֶׂה־פְּרִי אֲשֶׁר זַרְעוֹ־בוֹ
13 לְמִינֵהוּ וַיַּרְא אֱלֹהִים כִּי־טוֹב׃ וַיְהִי־עֶרֶב וַיְהִי־בֹקֶר
14 יוֹם שְׁלִישִׁי׃ וַיֹּאמֶר אֱלֹהִים יְהִי מְאֹרֹת בִּרְקִיעַ
הַשָּׁמַיִם לְהַבְדִּיל בֵּין הַיּוֹם וּבֵין הַלָּיְלָה וְהָיוּ לְאֹתֹת
15 וּלְמוֹעֲדִים וּלְיָמִים וְשָׁנִים׃ וְהָיוּ לִמְאוֹרֹת בִּרְקִיעַ
16 הַשָּׁמַיִם לְהָאִיר עַל־הָאָרֶץ וַיְהִי־כֵן׃ וַיַּעַשׂ אֱלֹהִים
אֶת־שְׁנֵי הַמְּאֹרֹת הַגְּדֹלִים אֶת־הַמָּאוֹר הַגָּדֹל לְמֶמְשֶׁלֶת
הַיּוֹם וְאֶת־הַמָּאוֹר הַקָּטֹן לְמֶמְשֶׁלֶת הַלַּיְלָה וְאֵת
17 הַכּוֹכָבִים׃ וַיִּתֵּן אֹתָם אֱלֹהִים בִּרְקִיעַ הַשָּׁמָיִם לְהָאִיר
18 עַל־הָאָרֶץ׃ וְלִמְשֹׁל בַּיּוֹם וּבַלַּיְלָה וּלֲהַבְדִּיל בֵּין הָאוֹר
19 וּבֵין הַחֹשֶׁךְ וַיַּרְא אֱלֹהִים כִּי־טוֹב׃ וַיְהִי־עֶרֶב וַיְהִי־
20 בֹקֶר יוֹם רְבִיעִי׃ וַיֹּאמֶר אֱלֹהִים יִשְׁרְצוּ הַמַּיִם שֶׁרֶץ
נֶפֶשׁ חַיָּה וְעוֹף יְעוֹפֵף עַל־הָאָרֶץ עַל־פְּנֵי רְקִיעַ הַשָּׁמָיִם׃

CAPVT PRIMVM.

1 IN principio creauit Deus cælum & terrã. 2 * Terra autem
A erat inanis & vacua: & tenebræ erant ſuper faciẽ abyſſi:
& ſpiritus Dei ferebatur ſu-
3 per aquas. * Dixitq; Deus, Fiat lux. Et facta eſt
4 lux. * Et vidit Deus lucem quòd eſſet bona: &
5 diuiſit lucem à tenebris. * Appellauitq; lucem
diem; & tenebras noctẽ. Factumq; eſt veſpere
6 & mane dies vnus. * Dixit quoque Deus, Fiat
firmamentũ in medio aquarum; & diuidat a-
7 quas ab aquis. * Et fecit Deus firmamentum,
diuiſitq; aquas quæ erant ſub firmamento, ab
his quæ erant ſuper firmamentũ. Et factum eſt
8 ita. * Vocauitq; Deus firmamentũ, cælum: &
factum eſt veſpere, & mane dies ſecundus.
9 * Dixit verò Deus, Congregentur aquæ quæ
ſub cęlo ſunt, in locum vnum: & appareat ari-
10 da. Et factum eſt ita. * Et vocauit Deus aridã,
terram: congregationeſq; aquarum appellauit
11 maria. Et vidit Deus quòd eſſet bonum. * Et
B ait, Germinet terra herbã virentem & facien-
tem ſemen; & lignum pomiferũ faciens fructũ
iuxta genus ſuum, cuius ſemen in ſemetipſo ſit
12 ſuper terram. Et factũ eſt ita. * Et protulit terra
herbam virentẽ, & facientẽ ſemen iuxta genus
ſuũ; lignumq; faciens fructũ; & habens vnum-
quodq; ſementem ſecundũ ſpeciem ſuam. Et
13 vidit Deus quòd eſſet bonum. * Et factum eſt
14 veſpere & mane dies tertius. * Dixit autẽ Deus,
Fiant luminaria in firmamento cæli; & diui-
dant diem ac noctẽ; & ſint in ſigna & tẽpora
15 & dies & annos: * Vt luceãt in firmamẽto cæli,
16 & illuminent terrã. Et factum eſt ita. * Fecitq;
Deus duo luminaria magna: luminare maius,
vt præeſſet diei: & luminare minus, vt pręeſſet
17 nocti: & ſtellas. * Et poſuit eas Deus in firma-
18 mẽto cæli, vt lucerẽt ſuper terrã: * Et pręeſſent
diei ac nocti; & diuiderent lucem ac tenebras.
19 Et vidit Deus quòd eſſet bonũ. * Et factum eſt
20 veſpere, & mane dies quartus. * Dixit etiam
Deus, Producant aquæ reptile animæ viuentis,
& volatile ſuper terram ſub firmamento cæli.

תרגום אונקלוס

בְּקַדְמִין בְּרָא יְיָ יָת שְׁמַיָּא וְיָת אַרְעָא׃ 2 וְאַרְעָא הֲוָת צַדְיָא וְרֵיקַנְיָא וַחֲשׁוֹכָא עַל אַפֵּי תְהוֹמָא וְרוּחָא דַיְיָ מְנַשְּׁבָא עַל
אַפֵּי מַיָּא׃ 3 וַאֲמַר יְיָ יְהֵא נְהוֹרָא וַהֲוָה נְהוֹרָא׃ 4 וַחֲזָא יְיָ יָת נְהוֹרָא אֲרֵי טָב וְאַפְרֵשׁ יְיָ בֵּין נְהוֹרָא וּבֵין
חֲשׁוֹכָא׃ 5 וּקְרָא יְיָ לִנְהוֹרָא יְמָמָא וְלַחֲשׁוֹכָא קְרָא לֵילְיָא וַהֲוָה רְמַשׁ וַהֲוָה צְפַר יוֹמָא חַד׃ 6 וַאֲמַר יְיָ יְהֵא רְקִיעָא בִּמְצִיעוּת מַיָּא
וִיהֵא מַפְרֵשׁ בֵּין מַיָּא לְמַיָּא׃ 7 וַעֲבַד יְיָ יָת רְקִיעָא וְאַפְרֵשׁ בֵּין מַיָּא דְּמִלְּרַע לִרְקִיעָא וּבֵין מַיָּא דְּמִלְּעֵל לִרְקִיעָא וַהֲוָה כֵן׃ 8 וּקְרָא יְיָ
לִרְקִיעָא שְׁמַיָּא וַהֲוָה רְמַשׁ וַהֲוָה צְפַר יוֹם תִּנְיָן׃ 9 וַאֲמַר יְיָ יִתְכַּנְשׁוּן מַיָּא מִתְּחוֹת שְׁמַיָּא לַאֲתַר חַד וְתִתַּחְזֵי יַבֶּשְׁתָּא וַהֲוָה כֵן׃ 10 וּקְרָא
יְיָ לְיַבֶּשְׁתָּא אַרְעָא וּלְבֵית כְּנִישׁוּת מַיָּא קְרָא יַמֵּי וַחֲזָא יְיָ אֲרֵי טָב׃ 11 וַאֲמַר יְיָ תַּדְאֵי אַרְעָא דִּתְאָה עִסְבָּא דְּבַר זַרְעֵהּ מִזְדְּרַע אִילַן פֵּירִין עָבֵד
פֵּירִין לִזְנוֹהִי דְּבַר זַרְעֵהּ בֵּהּ עַל אַרְעָא וַהֲוָה כֵן׃ 12 וְאַפֵּיקַת אַרְעָא דִּתְאָה עִסְבָּא דְּבַר זַרְעֵהּ מִזְדְּרַע לִזְנוֹהִי וְאִילַן עָבֵד פֵּירִין דְּבַר זַרְעֵהּ
בֵּהּ לִזְנוֹהִי וַחֲזָא יְיָ אֲרֵי טָב׃ 13 וַהֲוָה רְמַשׁ וַהֲוָה צְפַר יוֹם תְּלִיתַאי׃ 14 וַאֲמַר יְיָ יְהוֹן נְהוֹרִין בִּרְקִיעָא דִשְׁמַיָּא לְאַפְרָשָׁא בֵּין יְמָמָא
וּבֵין לֵילְיָא וִיהוֹן לְאָתִין וּלְזִמְנִין וּלְמִמְנֵי בְהוֹן יוֹמִין וּשְׁנִין׃ 15 וִיהוֹן לִנְהוֹרִין בִּרְקִיעָא דִשְׁמַיָּא לְאַנְהָרָא עַל אַרְעָא וַהֲוָה כֵן׃ 16 וַעֲבַד יְיָ
יָת תְּרֵין נְהוֹרִין רַבְרְבִין יָת נְהוֹרָא רַבָּא לְמִשְׁלַט בִּימָמָא וְיָת נְהוֹרָא זְעֵירָא לְמִשְׁלַט בְּלֵילְיָא וְיָת כּוֹכְבַיָּא׃ 17 וִיהַב יָתְהוֹן יְיָ בִּרְקִיעָא
דִשְׁמַיָּא לְאַנְהָרָא עַל אַרְעָא׃ 18 וּלְמִשְׁלַט בִּימָמָא וּבְלֵילְיָא וּלְאַפְרָשָׁא בֵּין נְהוֹרָא וּבֵין חֲשׁוֹכָא וַחֲזָא יְיָ אֲרֵי טָב׃ 19 וַהֲוָה רְמַשׁ וַהֲוָה
צְפַר יוֹם רְבִיעַאי׃ 20 וַאֲמַר יְיָ יִרְחֲשׁוּן מַיָּא רִחֲשָׁא נַפְשָׁא חַיְתָא וְעוֹפָא דְּפָרַח עַל אַרְעָא עַל אַפֵּי אֲוִיר רְקִיעַ שְׁמַיָּא׃

Reliable texts attractively presented: the Plantin and Moretus publishing dynasty

Dirk Imhof

Plantin persuaded scientists and humanists to publish their work through him. He challenged them to publish new research, and distributed their books all over Europe. Plantin was a born networker, bringing together the most talented people: renowned authors and the best type cutters, compositors, printers, proofreaders and book illustration designers. He also had to lobby, travel and write entreaties, in order to get his books printed. The path of a publisher in the sixteenth century was not exactly a bed of roses.

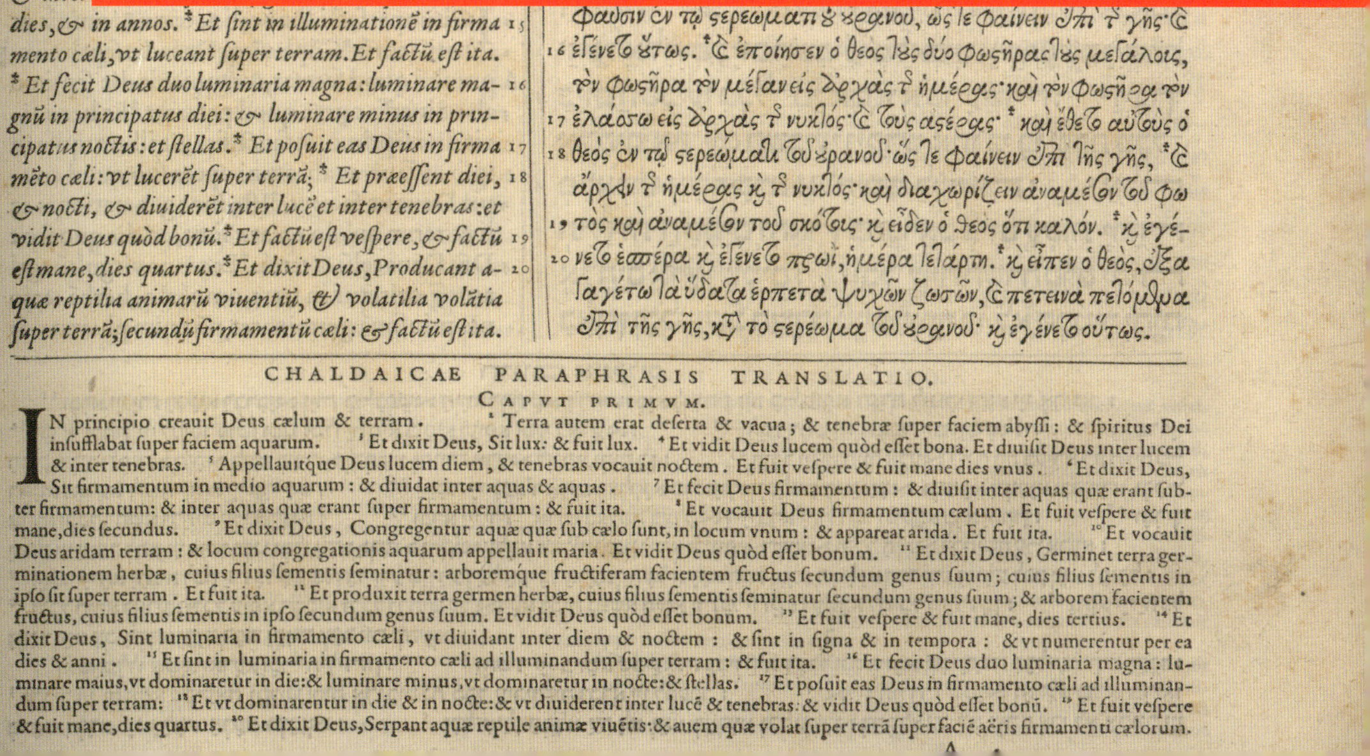
dies, & in annos. * Et ſint in illuminationē in firma 15
mento cæli, vt luceant ſuper terram. Et factū eſt ita.
* Et fecit Deus duo luminaria magna: luminare ma- 16
gnū in principatus diei: & luminare minus in prin-
cipatus noctis: et ſtellas. * Et poſuit eas Deus in firma 17
mēto cæli: vt lucerēt ſuper terrā; * Et præeſſent diei, 18
& nocti, & diuiderēt inter lucē et inter tenebras: et
vidit Deus quòd bonū. * Et factū eſt veſpere, & factū 19
eſt mane, dies quartus. * Et dixit Deus, Producant a- 20
quæ reptilia animarū viuentiū, & volatilia volātia
ſuper terrā; ſecundū firmamentū cæli: & factū eſt ita.

φαῦσιν ἐν τῷ στερεώματι τοῦ οὐρανοῦ, ὥστε φαίνειν ἐπὶ τῆς γῆς· καὶ
16 ἐγένετο οὕτως. * καὶ ἐποίησεν ὁ θεὸς τοὺς δύο φωστῆρας τοὺς μεγάλους,
τὸν φωστῆρα τὸν μέγαν εἰς ἀρχὰς τῆς ἡμέρας· καὶ τὸν φωστῆρα τὸν
17 ἐλάσσω εἰς ἀρχὰς τῆς νυκτός· καὶ τοὺς ἀστέρας· * καὶ ἔθετο αὐτοὺς ὁ
18 θεὸς ἐν τῷ στερεώματι τοῦ οὐρανοῦ· ὥστε φαίνειν ἐπὶ τῆς γῆς, * καὶ
ἄρχειν τῆς ἡμέρας καὶ τῆς νυκτός· καὶ διαχωρίζειν ἀναμέσον τοῦ φω-
19 τὸς καὶ ἀναμέσον τοῦ σκότους· καὶ εἶδεν ὁ θεὸς ὅτι καλόν. * καὶ ἐγέ-
20 νετο ἑσπέρα καὶ ἐγένετο πρωΐ, ἡμέρα τετάρτη. * καὶ εἶπεν ὁ θεός, ἐξα-
γαγέτω τὰ ὕδατα ἑρπετὰ ψυχῶν ζωσῶν, καὶ πετεινὰ πετόμενα
ἐπὶ τῆς γῆς, κατὰ τὸ στερέωμα τοῦ οὐρανοῦ· καὶ ἐγένετο οὕτως.

CHALDAICAE PARAPHRASIS TRANSLATIO.

CAPVT PRIMVM.

IN principio creauit Deus cælum & terram. [2] Terra autem erat deſerta & vacua; & tenebræ ſuper faciem abyſſi: & ſpiritus Dei inſufflabat ſuper faciem aquarum. [3] Et dixit Deus, Sit lux: & fuit lux. [4] Et vidit Deus lucem quòd eſſet bona. Et diuiſit Deus inter lucem & inter tenebras. [5] Appellauitque Deus lucem diem, & tenebras vocauit noctem. Et fuit veſpere & fuit mane dies vnus. [6] Et dixit Deus, Sit firmamentum in medio aquarum: & diuidat inter aquas & aquas. [7] Et fecit Deus firmamentum: & diuiſit inter aquas quæ erant ſubter firmamentum: & inter aquas quæ erant ſuper firmamentum: & fuit ita. [8] Et vocauit Deus firmamentum cælum. Et fuit veſpere & fuit mane, dies ſecundus. [9] Et dixit Deus, Congregentur aquæ quæ ſub cælo ſunt, in locum vnum: & appareat arida. Et fuit ita. [10] Et vocauit Deus aridam terram: & locum congregationis aquarum appellauit maria. Et vidit Deus quòd eſſet bonum. [11] Et dixit Deus, Germinet terra germinationem herbæ, cuius filius ſementis ſeminatur: arboremque fructiferam facientem fructus ſecundum genus ſuum; cuius filius ſementis in ipſo ſit ſuper terram. Et fuit ita. [12] Et produxit terra germen herbæ, cuius filius ſementis ſeminatur ſecundum genus ſuum; & arborem facientem fructus, cuius filius ſementis in ipſo ſecundum genus ſuum. Et vidit Deus quòd eſſet bonum. [13] Et fuit veſpere & fuit mane, dies tertius. [14] Et dixit Deus, Sint luminaria in firmamento cæli, vt diuidant inter diem & noctem: & ſint in ſigna & in tempora: & vt numerentur per ea dies & anni. [15] Et ſint in luminaria in firmamento cæli ad illuminandum ſuper terram: & fuit ita. [16] Et fecit Deus duo luminaria magna: luminare maius, vt dominaretur in die: & luminare minus, vt dominaretur in nocte: & ſtellas. [17] Et poſuit eas Deus in firmamento cæli ad illuminandum ſuper terram: [18] Et vt dominarentur in die & in nocte: & vt diuiderent inter lucē & tenebras: & vidit Deus quòd eſſet bonū. [19] Et fuit veſpere & fuit mane, dies quartus. [20] Et dixit Deus, Serpant aquæ reptile animæ viuētis: & auem quæ volat ſuper terrā ſuper faciē aëris firmamenti cælorum.

LETTRES
AMOVREVSES
DE MESSER GIRO-
LAM PARABOSQVE, AVEC
quelques autres ajoutées de nouueau à la
fin: reduitées de l'Italien en nôtre vul-
gaire François, Par Hubert Phi-
lippe de Villiers.

H.I.V.

EN ANVERS,
De l'Imprimerie de Christophle
Plantin.
1556.
AVEC PRIVILEGE.

Girolam Parabosque,
Lettres amoureuses,
Christophe Plantin,
1556: title page.

PP. 50–51: With the financial support of Philip II, Plantin realised his absolute masterpiece: the multilingual *Biblia polyglotta* or *Biblia Regia*. The work comprises eight parts: four parts with the Old Testament, one with the New Testament and three parts with 'Apparatus'. The whole enterprise took four years to complete: from 1568 to 1572. It brought international fame to Plantin.

FROM THE SIXTEENTH CENTURY THE publishing house known as the *Officina Plantiniana* was reputed to be one of the best in Europe. The Plantin label was associated with printing of the highest quality in terms of both content and form, on a par with that of Aldus and Paulus Manutius in Venice and Robert and Henri Estienne in Paris and Geneva. The Plantin name on the title page vouched for the high quality of paper, typefaces and printing and was synonymous with correct texts and the best illustrations. The combination of those factors was the key to the success of the *Officina Plantiniana*. However, that general recognition also engendered rivalry and spawned envy in the Low Countries and beyond. Rather than being an island, the publishing house constantly had to take into account what was happening round about: where was the greatest demand for their books, what trading rules, regulations and restrictions did they need to make allowances for, what were competitors in Antwerp, Paris and elsewhere doing? During the course of the publishing house's 300-year-long history, the directors made decisions which boosted its success, but there were also times when they chose a direction that led to the company's slow but inevitable decline. This rise and fall is part and parcel of what makes the story of the Plantin publishing house so exciting.

Obviously Plantin did not instantly produce the highest quality for which his printing house later became famous. It took work, perseverance and a long time to build his reputation. His first printed work was *La institutione di una fanciulla nata nobilmente* by the Italian author Giovanni Michele Bruto, produced for the Antwerp publisher Joannes Bellerus in 1555. In that period he often printed editions for other publishers. For example, in 1556 Antonius Meyerus' history of the counts of Flanders, the *Comites Flandriae*, was printed for Joannes Steelsius. The editions he published in those years were often works which had just appeared in Paris or Lyon. Knowing there was a good market for them, he could simply reprint them without too much risk; an unfair practice which he later condemned when other publishers reprinted his editions. The subjects of the books he published as a printer in those early years were very different from his later editions. For example, in 1556 he published popular works and

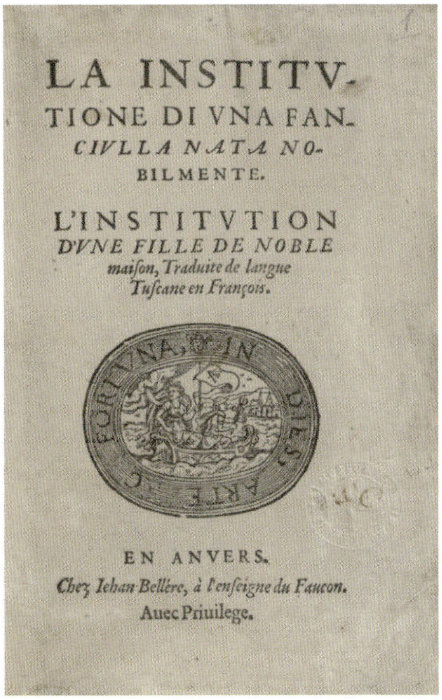
LA INSTITV-
TIONE DI VNA FAN-
CIVLLA NATA NO-
BILMENTE.
L'INSTITVTION
D'VNE FILLE DE NOBLE
maison, Traduite de langue
Tuscane en François.

EN ANVERS.
Chez Iehan Bellère, à l'enseigne du Faucon.
Auec Priuilege.

Giovanni Michele Bruto, *La institutione di una fanciulla nata nobilmente*, Christophe Plantin for Joannes Bellerus, 1555: title page.

new literature such as Girolam Parabosque's *Lettres amoureurses* and in 1557 Pierre de Ronsard's *Les amours*. Almost no editions of literary works appeared after these early years.

A large number of copies of these editions were destined for French booksellers. The Parisian dealer Martin le Jeune sometimes bought hundreds of copies. On a couple of occasions they divided the print run between the two of them: Plantin's name would appear on the title page in a number of copies and that of Le Jeune on others. In Paris Plantin also found financiers prepared to put up the money to print the works of Hendrik Niclaes. This Amsterdam dealer had founded the religious group 'Het huis der Liefde' (House of Love) which aspired to reconcile the differences between Catholics and Protestants. Plantin became closely involved with the group (for commercial or personal reasons) and Niclaes had provided him with the means to print his most important work, *Den spigel der gerechticheit* (Mirror of Justice). Moreover, he helped the printer Augustijn van Hasselt with the printing of other works by Niclaes until the former was forced to flee to Cologne for printing Protestant works.

Plantin also found himself in trouble with the law for printing Protestant works. The discovery of a Calvinist prayer book in his printing house forced him to take temporary

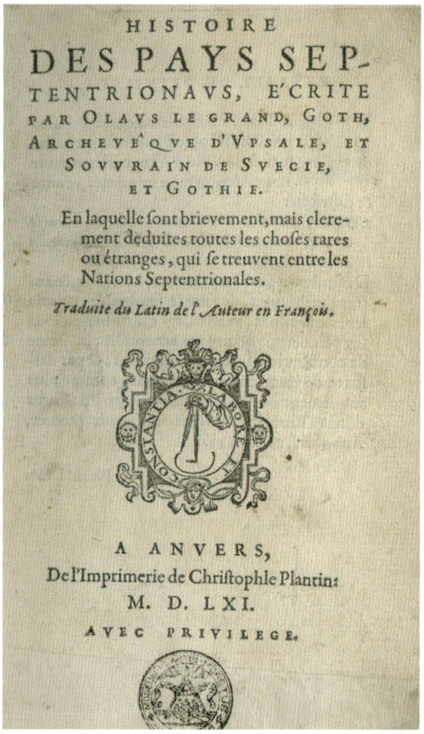

HISTOIRE
DES PAYS SEP-
TENTRIONAVS, E'CRITE
PAR OLAVS LE GRAND, GOTH,
ARCHEVEˆQVE D'VPSALE, ET
SOVVRAIN DE SVECIE,
ET GOTHIE.
En laquelle ſont brievement, mais clerement deduites toutes les choſes rares ou étranges, qui ſe treuvent entre les Nations Septentrionales.
Traduite du Latin de l'Auteur en François.
A ANVERS,
De l'Imprimerie de Chriſtophle Plantin.
M. D. LXI.
AVEC PRIVILEGE.

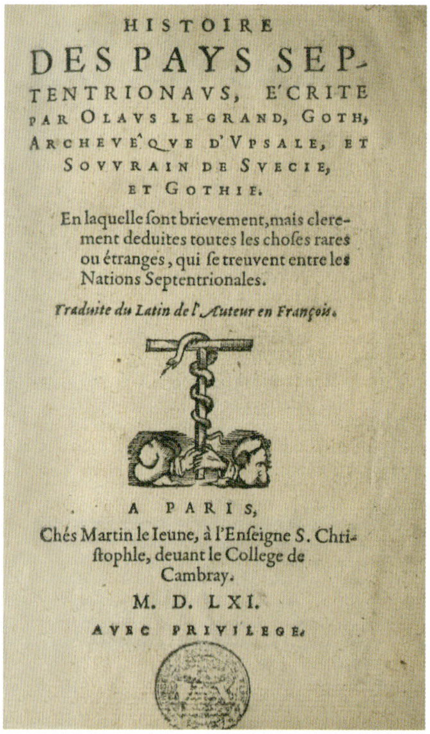

HISTOIRE
DES PAYS SEP-
TENTRIONAVS, E'CRITE
PAR OLAVS LE GRAND, GOTH,
ARCHEVEˆQVE D'VPSALE, ET
SOVVRAIN DE SVECIE,
ET GOTHIE.
En laquelle ſont brievement, mais clerement deduites toutes les choſes rares ou étranges, qui ſe treuvent entre les Nations Septentrionales.
Traduite du Latin de l'Auteur en François.
A PARIS,
Chés Martin le Ieune, à l'Enſeigne S. Chriſtophle, deuant le College de Cambray.
M. D. LXI.
AVEC PRIVILEGE.

Olaus Magnus, *Histoire des pays septentrionaus*, 1561. Part of the print run of this edition had Plantin's imprint on the title page, and the other part had the imprint of the Parisian publisher Martin le Jeune. Left, the title page with the Plantin imprint; right, with the imprint of Le Jeune.

Christoffel van Sichem,
Portrait of Hendrik Niclaes.

PP. 56–57: Signature of Plantin and his partners on the deed of foundation of the partnership in 1567.

refuge in Paris. However, nothing could be pinned on him and in 1563 he was able to return to Antwerp, but only to find that his entire company had been sold by public auction.
At this he formed a partnership with several wealthy Antwerp merchants to rebuild his company. The partnership was dissolved earlier than anticipated when his Protestant partners fled before the arrival of the Duke of Alva.
After that Plantin put his money on the Catholic rulers. On the one hand he was able to persuade King Philip II of Spain to fund a prestigious new publication of the polyglot Bible, the *Biblia regia* or King's Bible, and on the other hand he managed to net large orders for supplying revised Catholic liturgical works and prayer books.
The cardinals present at the Council of Trent decided that from then on all the liturgical works and prayer books should be standardized throughout the Catholic Church. It was no longer acceptable for one text to be used in the celebration of mass in one diocese, while another diocese used another text. Texts were carelessly printed and riddled with mistakes and printers sometimes used one Bible edition and sometimes another when quoting from the Scripture. Special commissions set to work, tackling first the breviary (the prayer book for priests) which after 1568 could only be printed if it conformed to the new approved edition that was printed in Rome. The missal (the book of prayers used during mass) followed in 1570 and in 1572 the preeminent prayer book for the layman, the *Officium beatae Mariae Virginis* or The Hours of Our Lady. It goes without saying that it was a huge task for a printer to print all these books for the whole of the Catholic Church.

Bien entendu toutefois questant finie ladite compagnie il pourra reprendre ses matrices
et les tenir pour soy sans estre en rien tenu pour icelles a ladite compagnie
Mais les matrices de brieu retourneront audit de bomberghe sans q la compagnie en
ait part quelconq
Item veu que pour le fait de ladite imprimerie on a chacun jour affaire de vieux linges
de feu dutensiles de menage des lessives et autres necessitez Est content ledit
plantin quil luy soit ordonne cincquante florins par an
Item tout le proffit qui ensuivra les frais preallablement deduitz sera reparty
entre lesditz compagnons a vng chacun pro ratta de sa mise sans fraude ou
malengin quelconq

Davantage estant finie ladite compagnie chacun des compagnons prendra en
payement tant de son capital mis comme des proffitz ensuiviz toutes telles
marchandises livres papiers deniers et debtes qui alors seront trouvez en
estre ne soit quaucun pact ou conventions expresses desditz compagnons fussent
trouvez au contraire
Item durant ladite compagnie ledit plantin ne pourra demeurer pleige ou
respondant pour personne quelconqz sans lexpres avis et consentement desditz
compagnons
Aussi il ne pourra fier a personne pour somme quelle puisse estre plus que la somme
de deux cens escus a la fois sil nestoit par le conseil et consentement dudit cornille de bombergh
Item sera repartie ladite compagnie en six portions egalles desquelles ledit cornille de
bomberghe retiendra pour soy et ledit plantin les trois portions —— 3 portion
Mr charles de bomberghe vne portion —— 1 portion
Mr Johannes goropius bekanus vne portion —— 1 portion
Sr Jaques de scotti vne portion —— 1 portion
6 portions

Davantage est expressement declaire que chacun des compagnons estant requis par
ledit cornille de bomberghe a mettre sa ratte part de ce qui sera necessaire pour
entretenir le train de ladite compagnie Icelluy le fera sans soy faire autrement
trop solliciter ne delayer et en cas de refus ou de dilation de trois mois du
parfournissement pourront les autres compagnons fournir la somme et ainsi
demourera ledit compagnon hors de la societe susdite de maniere quil ne pourra
plus rentrer Et sera quant et quant tenu et contraint de prendre en payement
pour ce quil y aura mis toutes telles marchandises comme livres imprimez
papiers fontes des lettres deniers et debtes qui seront alors trouvez procedez
de ladite compagnie sans quil puisse contraindre la compagnie de pouvoir
demourer oultre le gre desditz compagnons
Oultre est declaire que si durant le terme de ceste compe les monnoies fussent
haulsees ou rabaissees de leur cours et pris ordinaire Le tout sera au prouffit
et dommage de ladite compagnie
Item encores est tres expressement specifie que si durant le temps de ces huit annees
aucun desditz compagnons allat de vie a trespas Ladite compagnie au respect
du defunct sera expiree et finie et rendront alors les autres compagnons
compte et reliqua selon la teneur de cedit contract aux hoirs dudit defunct
ou aux tuteurs et curateurs diceux lesquelz tuteurs ou curateurs dudit
defunct seront contraints de se contenter du devoir desditz compagnons sans
plus avoir part a ladite compe ne fust quilz feissent autre accord ensemble

Encore est declaire par le commun accordt et expresse volonte desditz compaignons tous ensemble et chacun apart que sy aucun des hoirs ou tuteurs et curateurs diceulx ne vouloit ou vouloient se contenter des comptes a eux donnez par les aultres compaignons que non obstant les contestations ou malcontentement desditz hoirs ou tuteurs et curateurs diceulx ilz ne pourront contraindre les aultres compaignons de venir en justice et ce sous peine de deux cens escus dor en or laquelle peine veullent tous les compaignons susditz ensemble et chacun deulx pour sy et ses hoirs leurs tuteurs et curateurs contrevenantz a ceste presente escriture quelle soit levee des biens estans en ladite compagnie sans se pouvoir aider dexception quelconque soit telle quelle puisse estre et ce sans dol fraude ou circonvention aucune

Et pour approbation et ratification de tout ce que dessus on a fait cinq instrumens tous dune teneur souscris et soubsignez des mains desditz compaignons dont ung chacun a le sien, voulans et ordonnans lesditz compagnons que cest instrument ou escriture ait telle et sy grande vigeur et authorite comme sil estoit passe par devant eschevins de ceste ville damiens ou sil estoit fait et stipule dung notaire authenticque et comme aiant toutes les solemnitez legalles a ce requises se soumettans volontairement a lexecution de tout ce quest specifie cy dessus, Renoncans quant et quant a toutes cavillations relevemens et exceptions de droit tant generalles que especialles soient de telle authorite ne vigeur quelles pourroient estre ou de quelconque maniere que lesditz compaignons leurs hoirs tuteurs ou curateurs se pourroient ou vouldroient aider Le tout en parolle dhomme de bien sans dol fraude ou malengin quelconque

Fait en amiens ce xxvi[e] du mois de novembre au logis dudit m[r] Charles de bomberghe Lan de grace xv[c] lxiii

Je Jean Goropius Becanus appreuve tout ce quest cy dessus

Je Charles de bomberghe approuvue tout ce quest specifie cy dessus

Je Cornelle de bombergue approuve tout ce quest specifie cy dessus

Jo Jac[o] Scotto afermo quanto di supra e scritto

Je Christophle Plantin approuve tout ce qui est contenu cy dessus.

At the same time it was a very lucrative assignment, not least because the market was guaranteed. Initially the contract went to Paulus Manutius, a publisher in Venice, who subcontracted the printing to other printers elsewhere in Europe. The contract for the Low Countries and areas to the north of the Alps was awarded to Plantin, who after a while stopped paying the fee to Manutius.

While printing the *Biblia Regia*, an enormous work of eight large, folio-size volumes, he also began printing the hundreds of breviaries and missals in different formats. He won the order to print these books for Spain as well. In the space of a few years Plantin's company expanded at a fast and furious pace. The number of printing presses increased from four in 1566 to sixteen in 1572. There were times when the company's growth seemed almost out of control.

Increasingly liturgical works became the mainstay of the Plantin publishing house. This was a profitable market and other publishers also tried to get in on the act, but Plantin garnered privileges from the authorities in Brussels which gave him total control of that market. Privileges for printed works had been a recognized practice in the Low Countries since the beginning of the sixteenth century.

Breviarium Romanum ex decreto sacrosancti concilii Tridentini restitutum, Christophe Plantin, 1569, 2nd edition. Example with handwritten corrections for a following edition.

MISSALE ROMANVM,
EX DECRETO SACROSANCTI
Concilij Tridentini reſtitutum.
PII V. PONT. MAX.
IVSSV EDITVM.
ANTVERPIÆ,
Ex officina Chriſtophori Plantini,
Prototypographi Regij.
M. D. LXXIII.
Cum Priuilegiis Pont. Max. & Regis Catholici.

Missale Romanum ex decreto sacrosancti concilii Tridentini restitutum, Christophe Plantin, 1573. Example with corrections for the editions for Spain.

PP. 60–61: Georges de la Hèle, Orlando Lassus, Cyprianus de Rore, Thomas Crecquillon & Josquin des Prez, *Octo missae quinque, sex et septem vocum*, Antwerp, Christophe Plantin, 1578.

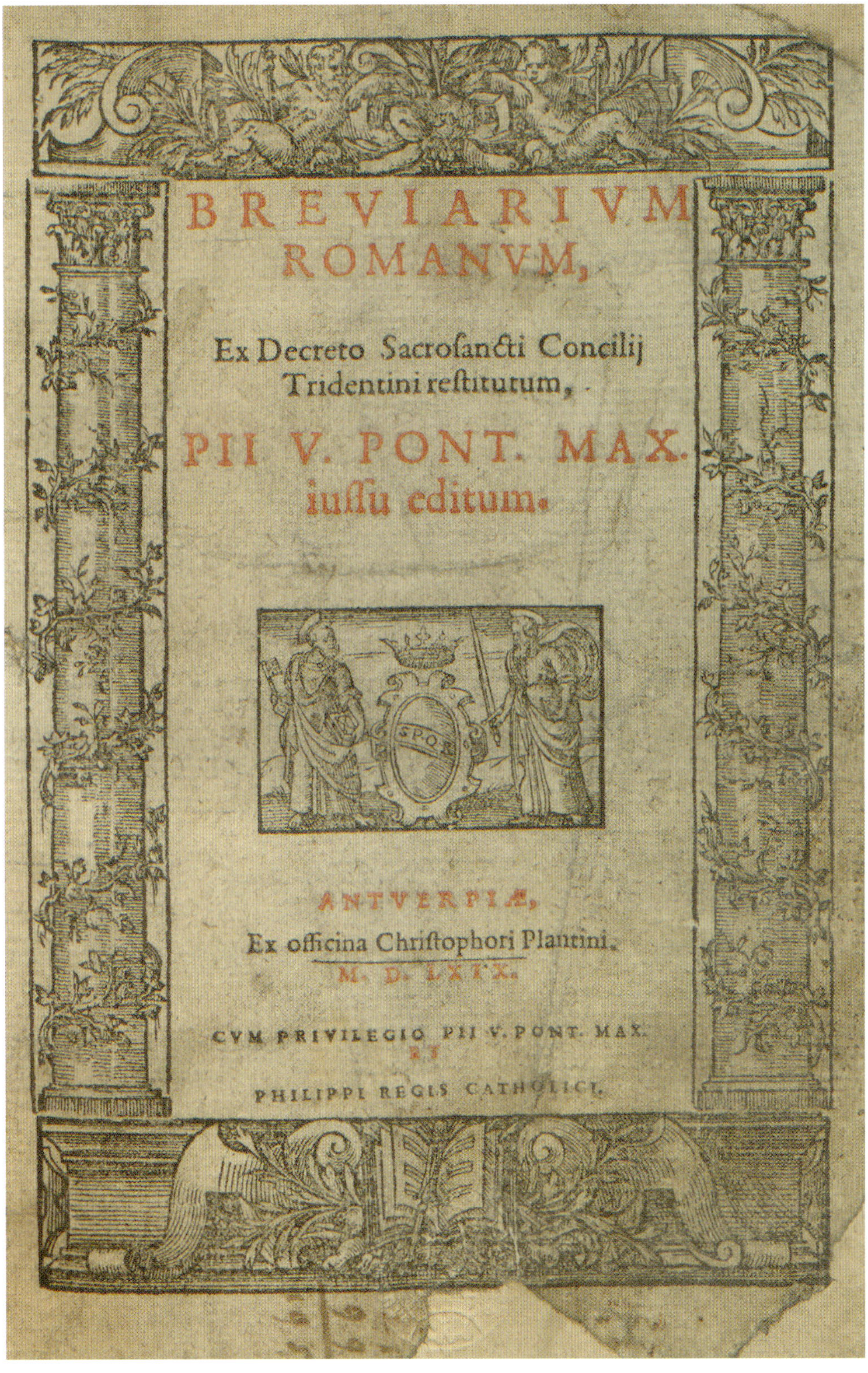

BREVIARIVM
ROMANVM,

Ex Decreto Sacrosancti Concilij
Tridentini restitutum,

PII V. PONT. MAX.
iussu editum.

ANTVERPIÆ,
Ex officina Christophori Plantini.
M. D. LXIX.

CVM PRIVILEGIO PII V. PONT. MAX.
ET
PHILIPPI REGIS CATHOLICI.

SVPERIVS.
Atrem omnipotẽtem, factorẽ cæ li & ter-
ræ, vi ſi bi li um omnium. Et in vnum
Dominum Ieſum Chriſtum, Fi li um De i
TENOR.
A ctorem cæ- li & ter ræ, vi-
ſi bi li um o- mnium & in ui ſi-
bilium. Et in vnũ Dominum Ieſum Chriſtum, Fi lium De-
BASIS.
Actorem cæ li & terræ, vi ſi bi li um
o- mnium & in ui ſi bi li um,

ALTVS.
P
Atrem omni- poten-
tem, factorem cæli & terræ, vi-
si bi li um omnium & in ui si bi li um. Et in vnum Do- mi-
num Iesum Christum, Fi li um De- i, Fi li um
TENOR 2ª.
P
Atrem omni- po-
ten- tem, factorem cæ li & ter ræ, vi-
si bi li um o- mnium & in ui si bi- lium. Et
in vnum Dominum Iesum Chri- stum, Fi li um De i
BASIS.
Et in vnũ Dominum Iesum Chri- stum, Fi li um De-

When a publisher (or an author) was granted a privilege for a particular edition, it was against the law for other publishers to print the work or to sell it in the jurisdiction of the authority that had issued the privilege. That ban applied for a number of years or for an indeterminate period. It meant that the publisher could sell his books without having to worry that another publisher would reprint the same works and undercut him. At the same time it allowed the government to control what was published because Emperor Charles v had promulgated a law which stated that before applying for a privilege, a publisher first had to receive the endorsement of a Catholic censor that the book contained nothing that was at variance with the Catholic doctrine. Though the Antwerp printer Emanuel Philippus Trognesius had also received a license from the Pope in 1568 authorizing him to print the breviary, Plantin enjoyed privileges granted by the Council of Brabant and the Secret Council (Geheime Raad) which thwarted Trognesius' plan and prevented him competing with him in that area.

When Plantin's son-in-law Jan I Moretus took over the printing house in 1589, one of the first things he did was apply for a privilege which would confirm that he would enjoy the same privileges as his predecessor Plantin. When Plantin died, several competitors had hoped that they, too, would then be able to publish some of the profitable Plantin editions. Jan Moretus was granted his privilege on 16 May 1591 which meant that only he could print Plantin's earlier editions. However, he still had to appeal to the Council of Brabant on several occasions when his exclusivity on liturgical works was violated. Plantin's other son-in-law, Gillis Beys, also a printer, believed he had been treated unjustly because Plantin's printing and publishing house had gone to Jan Moretus alone. The conflict between the two sons-in-law only ended when the Council of Brabant found Beys to be in the wrong and he returned to Paris. Several years later, other Antwerp printers also tried to break Jan Moretus' monopoly on the printing of liturgical works by printing a missal. Their endeavours had the open support of the bishops of the Southern Netherlands who believed that Jan Moretus was abusing his monopoly by charging too high a price for his books. Again the Council of Brabant ruled in Jan Moretus' favour.

Anonymous, *Portrait of Gillis Beys*, oil on panel.

All sorts of languages were printed here, such as Hebrew, Old Syrian, Arabic and Samaritan. Very few printers took up the challenge of printing these languages, as their letters were hard to come by. Whoever had the stamps or matrices required for casting the letters controlled the market. So Plantin tried to buy up as many stamps as possible. His Hebrew stamps and matrices are still kept here today. The Arabic stamps went to the branch in Leiden, as Raphelengius printed several Arabic books. Balthasar I Moretus tried to buy back the Arabic stamp set from his relatives, but his attempt failed.

Guillaume I Le Bé, *Letter stamps for 'Gros Hebreu Fort Gros'*, 1559.

PP. 64–65: Abraham Ortelius, *Théâtre de l'Univers*, Christophe Plantin for Abraham Ortelius, 1587. In 1570, Ortelius was the first person to collect all the known maps of the world in one book: the first atlas. Nearly forty editions of this atlas were published in seven languages. For his atlas, Ortelius used maps by different cartographers and made them all the same size.

TYPVS ORB
AMERICA SIVE IN DIA NOVA. Ao 1492. a Christophoro Colombo nomine regis Castellæ primum detecta.
CIRCVLVS ARCTICVS.
TROPICVS CANCRI
CIRCVLVS AEQVINOCTIALIS
TROPICVS CAPRICORNI.
CIRCVLVS ANTARCTICVS.
MAR DEL ZVR
MAR DEL NORT
EL MAR PACIFICO
Hanc continentem Australem, nonnulli Magellanicam regionem ab eius inventore nuncupant.
Nova Guinea nuper inventa que an sit insula an pars continentis Australis incertu est
OCCI
DENS.
Noua Francia
Chilaga
Florida
Peru.
Brasil
Caribana.
Chile.
Terra del Fuego.
TERRA AVSTR
QVID EI POTEST VIDERI MAGNVM IN
OMNIS, TOTIVSQVE MVNDI N
Cum privilegio.

TERRARVM
Mongol.
Tartaria
EVROPA
ASIA
Turcheſtan
China.
Perſia
India orientalis.
Arabia.
AFRICA.
Nubia
Manicongo.
MAR DI INDIA
Vaſtiſsimas hic eſſe regiones ex M. Pauli Ven: et Lud: Vartomanni ſcriptis peregrinationibus conſtat.
Pſitacorum regio,
S NONDVM COGNITA.
VS HVMANIS, CVI AETERNITAS
SIT MAGNITVDO. CICERO:

With the introduction of a new papal regulation, from the beginning of the seventeenth century other printers could also print liturgical works. However, the ascendancy of the Plantin publishing house was such that they never posed a real threat.

This pattern repeated itself several times after the death of Jan I Moretus in 1610. His successors, Balthasar I and Jan II, were granted a new papal licence in 1611 and a privilege confirming that they would continue to have recourse to the same privileges as their father. Despite this privilege, the Antwerp printers Jan II van Keerberghen and Hieronymus II Verdussen joined forces in the *Societas librorum officii ecclesiastici* which in 1620 tried to end the Plantin supremacy. But even now the Plantin publishing house proved insuperable.

Plantin and the Moretuses were very proud of the quality of their products. However, that pride sometimes verged on arrogance. When a new antiphonary had to be printed in 1609, Moretus suggested to the archbishop that he was the man to do it. The archbishop could safely entrust smaller

Phle par la grace de Dieu Roy de Castille d'Arragon de Leon des deux

General charter given to Jan Moretus by the Secret Council in 1591.

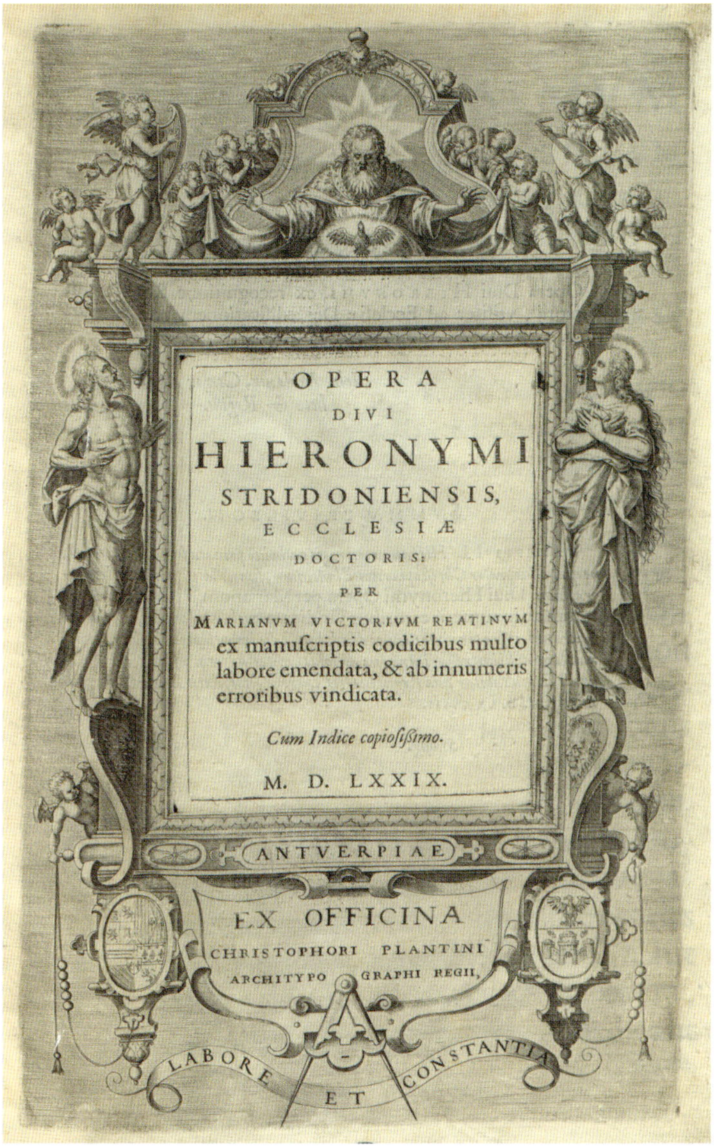
OPERA
DIVI
HIERONYMI
STRIDONIENSIS,
ECCLESIÆ
DOCTORIS:
PER
MARIANVM VICTORIVM REATINVM
ex manuſcriptis codicibus multo
labore emendata, & ab innumeris
erroribus vindicata.
Cum Indice copioſiſſimo.
M. D. LXXIX.
ANTVERPIAE
EX OFFICINA
CHRISTOPHORI PLANTINI
ARCHITYPOGRAPHI REGII.
LABORE ET CONSTANTIA

Hieronymus, *Opera*, Christophe Plantin, 1579, vol. I: title page.

format works for poor churches to other printers such as Joachim Trognesius, but the *Officina Plantiniana* could be the only contender for books for cathedrals. Two years earlier Jan Moretus had written to a canon in Mechelen saying that he was not afraid of the local competition; he only paid attention to what was happening in Paris. But, with an inevitable touch of histrionics, he added that the *Plantiniani* (Plantin's successors) would not give ground to Parisian publishers either. Balthasar I Moretus displayed an even greater sense of pride. When a priest who wanted him to print a book complained about the high cost, he retorted: 'I don't print for the same price as other printers, just as Rubens doesn't paint for the same price as other painters'. And while other booksellers often conducted trade by exchanging each others' books, he replied that he was in business not to swap books but to make a profit.

Though Bibles, liturgical works and prayer books occupied an important place in the list of Plantin and his early successors, scores of other publications on other subjects also appeared. The religious publications included voluminous editions by church fathers, numerous devotional and theological works and also saints' lives. This ratio increased from a third of Plantin's total production

The decimal system is Stevin's major work. *De Thiende* describes the application of decimal fractions in adding, subtracting, multiplying, dividing and calculating a square root. Stevin applies the decimal system to coins, square measures and measures of capacity, which are very useful for international trade. Nevertheless, his ideas will not be fully introduced until after the French Revolution.

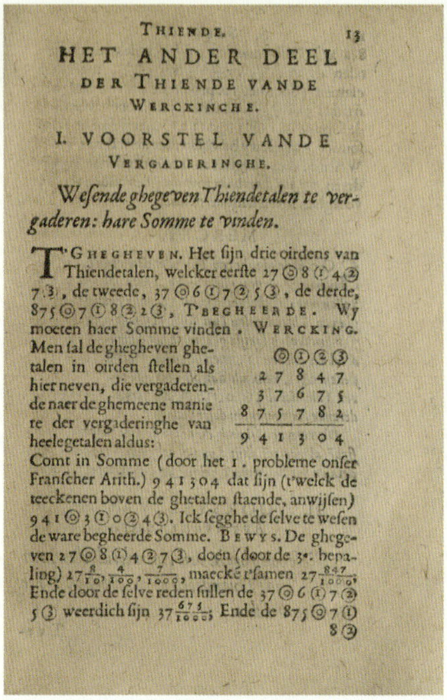

THIENDE. 13

HET ANDER DEEL
DER THIENDE VANDE
WERCKINCHE.

I. VOORSTEL VANDE
VERGADERINGHE.

Wesende ghegeven Thiendetalen te vergaderen: hare Somme te vinden.

T'GHEGHEVEN. Het sijn drie oirdens van Thiendetalen, welcker eerste 27⓪8①4②7③, de tweede, 37⓪6①7②5③, de derde, 875⓪7①8②2③, T'BEGHEERDE. Wy moeten haer Somme vinden. WERCKING. Men sal de gheghevenghe-talen in oirden stellen als hier neven, die vergaderende naer de ghemeene maniere der vergaderinghe van heelegetalen aldus:

⓪	①	②	③
27	8	4	7
37	6	7	5
875	7	8	2
941	3	0	4

Comt in Somme (door het 1. probleme onser Franscher Arith.) 941304 dat sijn (t'welck de teeckenen boven de ghetalen staende, anwijsen) 941⓪3①0②4③. Ick segghe de selve te wesen de ware begheerde Somme. BEWYS. De ghegeven 27⓪8①4②7③, doen (door de 3e. bepaling) $27\frac{8}{10}, \frac{4}{100}, \frac{7}{1000}$, maecke t'samen $27\frac{847}{1000}$. Ende door de selve reden sullen de 37⓪6①7②5③ weerdich sijn $37\frac{675}{1000}$; Ende de 875⓪7①8②

Simon Stevin,
De thiende, Leiden,
Christophe
Plantin, 1585.

to almost half under Jan I Moretus and to three-quarters on Balthasar I's death in 1641. Sciences accounted for barely 10% of the total in the period when Plantin headed up the publishing company. In particular, botanical works, such as the plant atlases of Rembert Dodoens, Carolus Clusius and Mathias Lobelius, and geographical works, like Abraham Ortelius' atlases, now also enjoyed fame. Works by classical authors and commentaries on their texts were another important group. In 1563 Plantin had started publishing classical authors in a small, cheap format (sedecimo), thereby treading in the footsteps of Aldus Manutius who had made a name for himself in Venice at the beginning of the sixteenth century for publishing classical authors in octavo rather than in large, but impractical and expensive folios and quartos. Moreover, in 1585 Plantin launched a series in an even smaller format (vigesimo-quarto or 24°), intended for travellers and impecunious students. Initially Jan Moretus went on printing the series in 16° (sedecim) in Antwerp, while his brother-in-law Franciscus I Raphelengius continued to publish the series in 24° (vigesimo-quarto) in Leiden. Eventually production of the series was discontinued in Antwerp.

Anonymous, *Potato plant*, watercolour drawing on paper, 1589.

Taratoufli a Philippo de Sivry
acceptum Viennae 26. Ianuarij
1588.
Papas Peruanum Petri Ciecae.

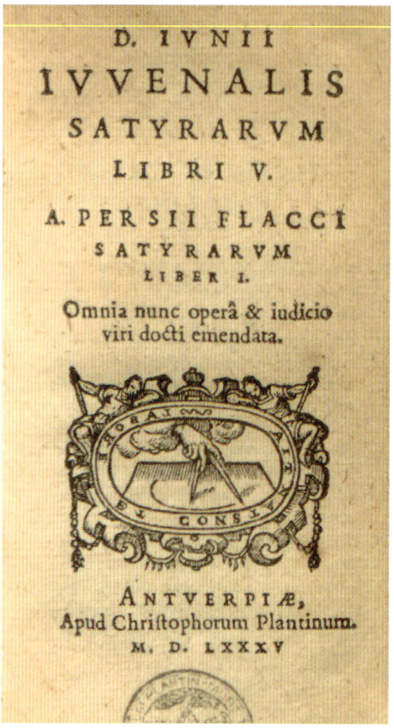

D. IVNII
IVVENALIS
SATYRARVM
LIBRI V.
A. PERSII FLACCI
SATYRARVM
LIBER I.
Omnia nunc operâ & iudicio
viri docti emendata.

ANTVERPIÆ,
Apud Christophorum Plantinum.
M. D. LXXXV

An edition by a classical author in 24° format: Juvenalis, *Satyrarum libri v*; Persius, *Satyrarum liber I*, [Leiden], Christophe Plantin, 1585: title page.

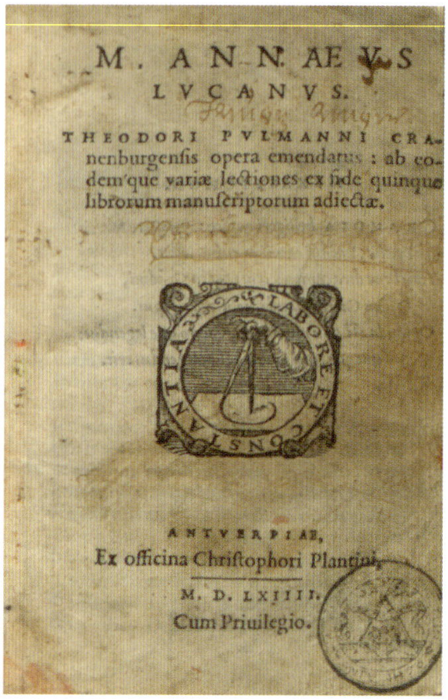

M. ANNÆVS
LVCANVS.
THEODORI PVLMANNI CRAnenburgensis opera emendatus: ab eodem'que variæ lectiones ex fide quinque librorum manuscriptorum adiectæ.

ANTVERPIÆ,
Ex officina Christophori Plantini.
M. D. LXIIII.
Cum Priuilegio.

An edition by a classical author in 16° format: Lucanus, [Opera] (ed. Theodorus Pulmannus), Christophe Plantin, 1564: title page.

This herbal is Dodoens' masterpiece, as well as being the synthesis of all his previous books. It has 965 pages and 1309 illustrations. Dodoens gives a systematic description of the plants and their origins, flowering season and use. The Moretuses continued to reprint the book up to 1644. It was even printed in a Japanese version in the eighteenth century.

PEMPTADIS SECVNDÆ LIB. II. 231

Leucoij bulbosi genus esse manifestum est: quod Hexaphyllum, non abs re, à sex floris foliolis cognominatur. Matthiolus cùm istud, tum superius Narcissi speciem facit, vt cap. De Narcisso scriptum est.

Tertium Leucoion bulbosum caule & foliis secundo simile est, maius tamen ac procerius: florem in singulis cauliculis non vnicum, sed quinque aut sex & particulatim quidem florentes, profert, alterius floribus forma & magnitudine per omnia similes. 3.

Est & hoc nobis hortense tantùm.

Non primo Vere, cum aliis duobus, sed multò pòst, Aprili videlicet demum mense, vnà cum Narcissis floret.

Violæ siue Leucoij bulbosi species haud dubiò quædam est, sed serotina.

Annumeratur verò & istis Leucoiis Bulbus quidam paruus, ex multis tunicis compactus, cui folia exeunt exilia, & cauliculus gracilis palmum altus, è cuius fastigio flosculus vnus aut alter dependet paruus, albidus, senum foliorum, Leucoio altero similis, sed minor multò, odore destitutus, & non Vere, sed Autumno prodiens.

At de facultatibus horum Leucoiorum nihil quod adferamus habemus, cùm à veteribus de iis nihil reperiatur proditum, & à recentioribus nihil quoque obseruatum.

De Tulipa. CAP. XXVII.

Tulipa. Tulipa cum semine.

EX bulbosorum florum numero & Tulipa est flos peregrinus; cuius differentes sunt species: quædam maiores sunt, aliæ minores.

Maioribus forma eadem satis omnibus est: folia eius bina aut terna, crassa, oblonga, lata, per oras subinde modicè reflexa, quæ cùm primum erumpunt, modicè rubere videntur, adulta verò albicāt: caulis inter ea exit pedalis aut paulò altior, cui vnicus flos insidet sursum spectans, è senis foliolis, patenti profundiori & aliquantulum angustioris oris cyatho, aut inuerso huius formæ pileo quodammodo similis, staminibus in medio croceis: color flori subinde luteus est, nonnunquam candidus, aliquando dilutè quasi purpureus, non rarò rubet: Varietatem autem in his non exiguam etiam admittit; margines siquidem foliorum, & non rarò vngues siue inferiores particulæ, aliter quàm foliola subinde colorata sunt: transeunt verò per 1.

V 2 hæc

Rembert Dodoens, *Stirpium historiae pemptades sex*, Christophe Plantin, 1583.

Tacitus, *Historiarum et Annalium libri,...de moribus Germanorum*, ed. Justus Lipsius, Christophe Plantin, 1574. In the first century, the Roman historian Tacitus wrote a history of Rome. This edition of Tacitus' works was Lipsius' first and most important work as a philologist. Tacitus' *Germania* describes the customs and traditions of the various Germanic races.

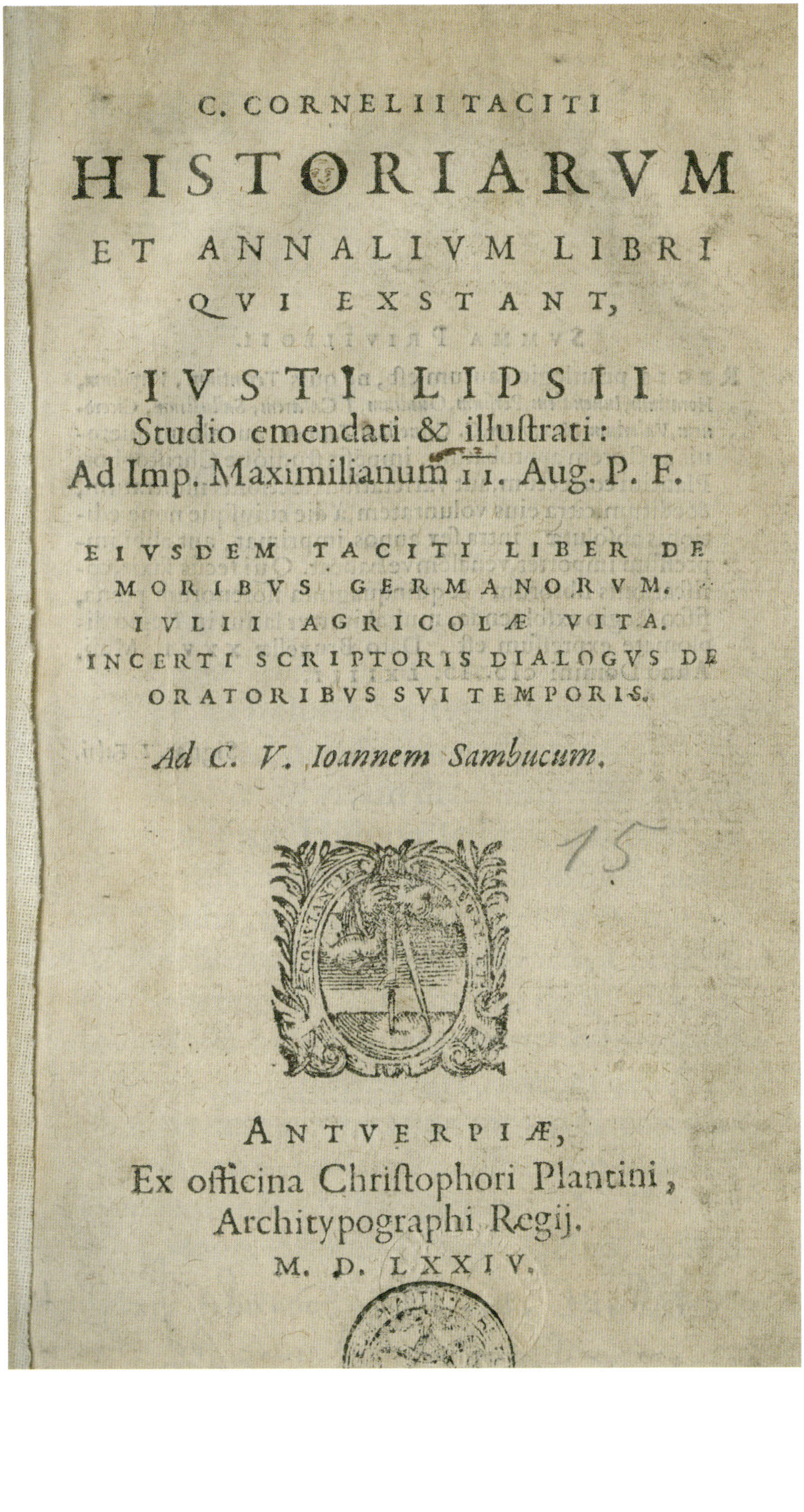

C. CORNELII TACITI
HISTORIARVM
ET ANNALIVM LIBRI
QVI EXSTANT,
IVSTI LIPSII
Studio emendati & illustrati:
Ad Imp. Maximilianum II. Aug. P. F.

EIVSDEM TACITI LIBER DE
MORIBVS GERMANORVM.
IVLII AGRICOLÆ VITA.
INCERTI SCRIPTORIS DIALOGVS DE
ORATORIBVS SVI TEMPORIS.

Ad C. V. Ioannem Sambucum.

15

ANTVERPIÆ,
Ex officina Christophori Plantini,
Architypographi Regij.
M. D. LXXIV.

Jan I and Balthasar I Moretus opted for large and luxurious editions which also proved highly successful, but were clearly intended for wealthier buyers. Lipsius' Seneca edition of 1605, a folio of almost 1,000 pages, was brought out again in 1615, 1632 and 1652. There was no more room on the Plantin publisher's list for the cheap, thin school editions with extra spacing for notes, which were printed in their thousands by Plantin and Jan Moretus until the beginning of 1590.

Works about history (both classical antiquity and events of the time), were well represented on the *Officina Plantiniana* list. There were several editions of Caesar Baronius' twelve-part history of the church, *Annales ecclesiastici*, under Jan I, Balthasar I and Balthasar II Moretus between 1589 and 1670, while Justus Lipsius with his numerous works about Roman history was the star author of both Jan and Balthasar I Moretus.

HERCVLES PALLAS VLYSSES

ZENO CLEANTHES

L. ANNÆI SENECÆ PHILOSOPHI OPERA, QVÆ EXSTANT OMNIA: A IVSTO LIPSIO emendata et Scholijs illustrata. Editio secunda, atque ab vltima LIPSI manu.

LABORE ET CONSTANTIA

ANTVERPIÆ, EX OFFICINA PLANTINIANA, apud Viduam et Filios Io. Moreti. M. DC. XV. Cum Priuilegijs Cæsareo et duorum Regum.

SENECA HONOS ET VIRTVS EPICTETVS

Seneca, *Opera, quae exstant omnia* (ed. Justus Lipsius), 1615.

Under Balthasar II most of the 112 non-religious editions were historical works (including accounts of contemporary events). Of particular note here is the large number of historical works by court physician to the Archduchess Isabella, antiquary and archaeologist Jean-Jacques Chifflet, the pivotal member of a French family that enjoyed close ties with the court in Brussels. He had already published

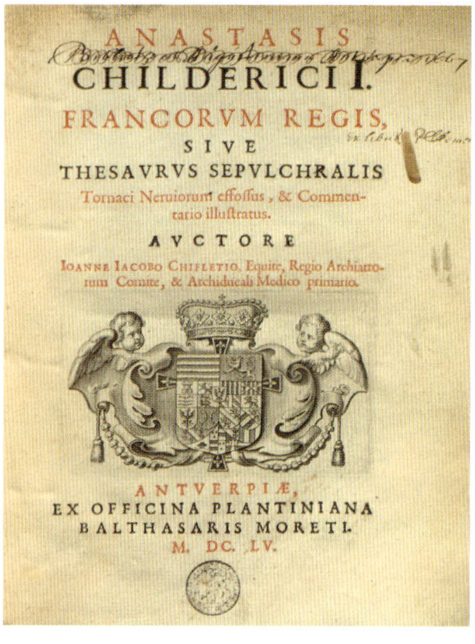

ANASTASIS CHILDERICI I. FRANCORVM REGIS, SIVE THESAVRVS SEPVLCHRALIS Tornaci Neruiorum effossus, & Commentario illustratus.

AVCTORE IOANNE IACOBO CHIFLETIO, Equite, Regio Archiatrorum Comite, & Archiducali Medico primario.

ANTVERPIÆ, EX OFFICINA PLANTINIANA BALTHASARIS MORETI. M. DC. LV.

Jean Jacques Chifflet, *Anastasis Childerici I Francorum regis, sive thesaurus sepulchralis Tornaci Nerviorum effosus*, Balthasar II Moretus, 1649.

works under Balthasar I Moretus. His works about the discovery of Childeric's grave and genealogical works in defence of the Spanish crown were among those published under Balthasar II. Some twenty literary works constitute the third large category of editions under Balthasar II Moretus. They are editions of Neo-Latin poetry by Jesuits such as Sidronius Hosschius and poems dedicated to sovereigns to commemorate their entry into the city of Antwerp, such as the works of Caspar Gevartius.

Rather surprisingly, in addition to all these hefty tomes, for many years the Plantin printing house also produced very simple printed matter. From 1579 Plantin had a contract

This allegory, which extols the *Officina Plantiniana*, was commissioned by Balthasar I Moretus in 1640. From left to right we see: Honour with the cornucopia as a symbol of prosperity, next to whom is a semi-nude Hercules, symbolising labour, who is holding the compass. Mercury, the god of commerce, is looking on while Constantia sits firmly on a chair with her hand on a pillar. At Athena's feet lie the books of wisdom: the product of the *Officina Plantiniana*.

Erasmus II Quellinus,
Labore et Constantia,
oil on canvas, c. 1640

Peter Paul Rubens, *Drawing for the title page of Bernardus Bauhusius, Epigrammata.*

with the city of Antwerp to print all its public announcements and ordinances. Orders issued by bailiff, burgomaster, aldermen and Antwerp city council ('*De Gheboden ende uutgeroepen by mijnen Heeren, Schouteth, Borgermeesteren, Schepenen, ende raedt der stadt van Antwerpen ...*') were printed on a single sheet and hung in public places in the city so that everyone could take note.

They covered the most diverse subjects relating to life in a city: illness, taxes, the cost of living, crime, war, etc. The Moretuses kept this contract until 1705. For several years Plantin also printed almanacs in large quantities in Dutch and French, in book form and as posters. However, next to none of the many thousands of copies he printed have survived. Lastly, the printing house also produced simple forms and documents such as receipts and passports.

Illustrations played an important role in making luxury editions more attractive and heightening their appeal. While continuing the collaboration with Theodore Galle's printing house begun by his father, Balthasar Moretus was also able to call upon an unrivalled artist to design title pages and illustrations for his books: Peter Paul Rubens. Instead of the customary, purely decorative illustrations for title pages, Rubens introduced a title page which was the visual translation of the book's content. By using allegories he evoked on the title page an image of what the reader could expect in the book. As their letters reveal, a title page for their book designed by Rubens proved a real bonus for authors of the time. The first book containing illustrations after designs by Rubens – a book about Roman antiquities by Filips Rubens, the painter's brother – had already appeared under Jan I Moretus in 1607,

Ban on brawls between young people, dated 20 October 1603 ('Al ist soo dat tot vele ende verscheyden reysen is verboden gheweest dat gheene iongers oft kinders hen en souden vervoor deren op de straten ... eenighe vergaderinge te maecken om te tuysschen').

PP. 76–77: *Gutenberg Bible*, Bamberg, Albrecht Pfister, before 1461. Plantin regularly bought expensive manuscripts and books by his competitors as reference works for his authors. The 36-line Bible was a milestone in printing history and is one of the most valuable treasures of the museum. In 1514, this Bible was in the monastery of the Augustinians in Antwerp. As they sympathised with the Protestants, there was a public sale of their goods, including this Bible. It is not known how the Bible ended up in Plantin's library.

Gheboden ende wt-gheroepen by mijnen Heeren, den Schouteth, Borgermeesteren, Schepenen ende Raedt der stadt van Antwerpen, op den xx. dagh Octobris, 1603.

AL ist soo dat tot vele eñ verscheyden reysen is verboden gheweest dat gheene iongers oft kinders hen en souden vervorderen op de straten / merckten / kerck-houen / vesten / oft andere publique plaetsen eenighe vergaderinge te maecken om te tuysschen / vechten / oft te balghen teghens malckanderen / eñ nochtans t'selue gheens-sins en is onder-houden gheweest noch achter-volght / in groote versmadenisse vander Justitien ende der gheboden deser Stadt: Soo ist datmen ander-werven wel scherpelijcken ghebiedt van weghen als bouen / dat egheen iongheren noch kinders voort-aen hen en vervorderen eenighe vergaderinghe langhs der straten op de kerck-houen / vesten / oft andere publicque plaetsen te maecken / om al-daer ghestockt / ghestaeft oft met steenen te gaen / oft teghens den anderen met steenen / gruys / oft anders-sins te worpen / onder hen te balghen / schreeuwen oft roepen / oft de ghelasen in stucken te worpen / malckanderen te slaen / steken oft te worpen / oft eenighe ongheschicktheydt te bedrijuen / daer deur lichtelijcken de passerende lieden souden moghen ghequetst oft eenigh on-gheval aen-ghedaen worden / d'welck oock oorsaecke soude gheuen van voordere beroerte. Opde verbeurte van hen opperste cleedt / eñ daer toe op arbitrale correctie vande geesselinghe / van te water ende te broode / oft aen een kake ghestelt te worden / oft anders-sins ghecorrigeert naer de gheleghentheydt vander saecken. Ende soo wat iongheren oft kinders hen laten vinden onder alsulcken vechtende oft balghende iongheren / ende hen terstondt uyt dien hoop niet en vertrecken / al ist oock soo dat sy niet mede gheworpen oft ghevochten en hebben / selen mede ghestraft worden als de veur-seyde vechtende iongheren. Ende soo wie bevonden wordt de veur-seyde vechtende iongheren daer toe te hebben op-ghestokt / ghesterckt / oft gheanimeert / sal noch hardder ghestraft worden / eenen anderen ten exemple. Ende selen daer-en-bouen d'ouders oft meesters vande selue kinders oft iongheren vervallen wesen inde pene van ses guldens / daer veur sy dadelijck selen gheexecuteert worden / al eer sy (ghecalengiert wesende) in rechte selen moghen ghehoort worden: al waer den Officier / s'Heeren dienaers / Prouosten vande Wacht / Wijck-meesters / ende publicque persoonen vol-comen ghelooue op hen simpel verclaeren sal ghegeuen worden. Ende selen oock ghehouden wesen de ghebroken ghelasen / ende andere schade den passanten oft huysen by de iongheren oft kinders aen-ghedaen zijnde te moeten betalen. De veur-seyde penen te bekeeren in drijen: d'een deel den Heere / d'ander den Officier oft den ghenen die d'exploict doen sal / ende het derde den huys-armen. Ende mids de vergaderinghe vande veur-seyde kinders nu ter tijdt meest gheschiedt deur de iongheren ende kinders die achter straeten zijn loopende om hout ende mutsaert / om Sinte Martens vier te maecken / &c. Soo ist dat-men ghebiedt wel scherpelijcken van wegen als bouen / dat egheen iongheren / kinders oft andere en selen moghen om-gaen achter straeten roepende oft singhende om hout te hebben om Sinte Martens vier te maecken / oft eenighe vergaderinghe te doen: maer sal van weghen de Magistraet gheordonneert worden sekeren dagh als de ghebueren selen moghen eenighe vieren maecken om de locht te purgeren ende de corruptien vande stadt wech te nemen. Verbiedende ins-ghelijcks dat als al-sulcke vieringhe sal gheschieden / dat de iongheren oft kinders daer by niet en selen moghen staen ghestockt / ghestaeft / oft met steenen worpen / oft eenighe onghetijdigheydt voortstellen / op ghelijcke pene.

H. de Moy.

uicē cū scribis dicebant. Alios
saluos fecit: seipsū non potest
saluū facere. Cristus rex israhel.
descendat nunc de cruce: ut vide-
amus et credamus. Et qui cū eo
crucifixi erāt cōuiciabant ei. Et
facta hora sexta: tenebre facte
sunt per totā terram usq; in ho-
rā nonā. Et hora nona excla-
mauit ihesus voce magna di-
cens. Heloy. heloy lema sabac-
tani. Quod est interpretatū. Deus me-
us. deus meus: ut quid dereliquis-
ti me. Et quidā de circūstantibus
audiētes dicebāt. Ecce heliam
vocat. Currēs autē unus et im-
plens spongiā aceto. circūpo-
nensq; calamo: potū dabat ei
dicens. Sinite: videamus si veni-
at helias ad deponēdū eū. Ihesus
autē emissa voce magna expi-
rauit. Et velum templi scissum
est in duo: a summo usq; deor-
sum. Videns autē centurio qui
ex aduerso stabat. quia sic clamās
expirasset: ait. Vere homo hic
filius dei erat. Erāt autē et muli-
eres de lōge aspiciētes: inter quas
erat maria magdalene. ⁊ mari-
a iacobi minoris. ⁊ ioseph ma-
ter. ⁊ salome: ⁊ cum esset ī gali-
lea sequebantur eū ⁊ ministra-
bāt ei: et alie multe que simul
cū eo ascenderāt iherosolimā.
Et cū iam sero esset factū. quia
erat parasceue quod est ante sab-
batū. venit ioseph ab arimathi-
a nobilis decurio: qui et ipse erat
expectās regnū dei. Et audacter
introiuit ad pilatū: ⁊ petijt cor-
pus ihesu. Pilatus autē mira-
batur si iam obisset. Et accersi-
to centurione: interrogauit eū si
iā mortuus esset. Et cū cogno-
uisset a centurione: donauit cor-
pus ioseph. Ioseph autē merca-
tus sindonem. et deponēs eum
inuoluit sindone: et posuit eū
in monumēto quod erat excisum
de petra: et aduoluit lapidē ad
ostiū monumēti. Maria mag-
dalene et maria ioseph aspicie-
bāt ubi poneretur. Capitulum xvi.

Et cum transisset sabbatū:
maria magdalene et ma-
ria iacobi ⁊ salome emerunt a-
romata: ut venientes ungerent
ihesum. Et valde mane una sab-
batorum. veniunt ad monumentū:
orto iam sole. Et dicebāt ad in-
uicē. Quis revoluet nobis la-
pidem ab ostio monumenti? Et
respicientes viderūt revolutū la-
pidē. Erat quippe magnus valde.
Et introeuntes in monumentū
viderunt iuuenem sedentem in
dextris coopertum stola candida:
et obstupuerūt. Qui dicit illis.
Nolite expauescere. Ihesum queri-
tis nazarenū. crucifixū: surrex-
it: nō est hic. Ecce locus: ubi po-
suerunt eum. Sed ite dicite dis-

diſcipulis eius et petro: q̄a precedet
vos in galileā. Ibi eum videbi-
tis: ſicut dixit vobis. At ille ex-
euntes fugerūt de monumēto.
Invaſerat eñi eas tremor ⁊ pa-
vor: et nemini quicq̄ȝ dixerunt.
Timebāt eñi. Surgēs aūt ihe-
ſus mane p̄ma ſabbati appa-
ruit p̄mo marie magdalene:
de qua eiecerat ſeptem demonia.
Illa vadens nūciavit hiis. qui
cum eo fuerāt lugentibȝ et flen-
tibȝ: ⁊ illi audiētes q̄a viveret ⁊
viſus eſſet ab ea: nō crediderūt.
Poſt hec aūt duobȝ ex hiis am-
bulātibȝ oſtenſus eſt in alia ef-
figie eūtibȝ in villā: et illi eūtes
nūciaverūt ceteris: nec illis cre-
diderūt. Noviſſime aūt recūbē-
tibȝ illis undecim apparuit: ⁊ ex-
probravit incredulitatē eoꝝ ⁊
duritiā cordis: q̄a hiis qui vide-
rāt eum reſurrexiſſe nō credide-
runt. Et dixit eis. Euntes ī mū-
dum univ̄ſum: p̄dicate euāge-
liū omī creature. Qui crediderit
et baptizatus fuit. ſalvus erit:
qui vero nō crediderit. condemna-
bitur. Signa aūt eos q̄ credide-
rint hec ſequētur. In noīe meo
demonia eiciēt: linguis loquēt
novis: ſerpētes tollēt. Et ſi mor-
tiferū q̄d biberit: non eis noce-
bit. Sup egros manus īpo-
nent: et bene habebūt. Et dn̄s
quidē ihc̄ poſtq̄ȝ locutus ē eis.

aſſumptus eſt in celū: ⁊ ſedet a
dextris dei. Illi aūt p̄fecti p̄dica-
verūt ubiq̄ȝ: dn̄o cooperante et
ſermonē cōfirmāte: ſequentibȝ
ſignis. Explicit ewangeliū ſcd̄m
marcū. Incipit p̄fatio bti ieronimi
p̄sbiteri in evangelium ſe-
cundum. Lucam.

LUcas ſirus. natio-
ne anthiocenſis. ar-
te medicus. diſcipu-
lus apoſtoloꝝ. poſ-
tea paulū ſecutus uſq̄ȝ ad cōfeſ-
ſionem eius ſerviens dn̄o ſine
crimine: nam neq̄ȝ uxorem un-
q̄ȝ habuit neq̄ȝ filios: ſeptuagi-
ta et quatuor ānoꝝ obiit in bi-
thinia. plenus ſpiritu ſancto.
Qui cum iā ſcripta eſſent. evan-
gelia. per matheū quidē in iude-
a. p marcū aūt in italia: ſācto
inſtigante ſpiritu in achaie
ptibȝ hoc ſcripſit evangelium:
ſignificans etiā ipſe in p̄ncipio
āte ſuū alia eſſe deſcripta. Cui
extra ea que ordo euāgelice diſ-
poſitionis expoſcit. ea maxime
neceſſitas laboris fuit: ut p̄mū
grecis fidelibȝ omī p̄phetatione
venturi in carnē dei xp̄i mani-
feſtata humanitate ne iudaicis
fabulis attenti: in ſolo legis de-
ſiderio tenerent̄: vel hereticis fa-
bulis ⁊ ſtultis ſollicitationibus
ſeducti exciderent a veritate ela-

Peter Paul Rubens, *Design for the printer's mark of Christophe Plantin for the title page of Lipsius Opera Omnia*, 1637, oil sketch.

immediately after Rubens' return to Antwerp from Italy. After that and until the late 1630s Rubens also helped make new designs for illustrations in missals and breviaries, philological, literary and scientific works, etc.

The luxurious editions of liturgical works were admired all over Europe. Through the agency of the Spanish Jesuit Philippus de Peralta, the Moretuses won important contracts for supplying Spain and the Spanish colonies with their editions. This led to the resumption of the export of large numbers of liturgical works from Antwerp to Spain which accounted for an ever-increasing share of the Officina's total output.

Since Plantin's time the *Officina Plantiniana* had made a practice of dividing a part of the print run of illustrated liturgical editions into copies with woodcuts and copies with engravings. This way they were able to cater for different categories of purchaser: those who wanted a cheap copy bought a copy with woodcuts and those who preferred a copy with more refined illustrations, purchased a more expensive copy with engravings. The process of illustrating the same text with either

The great Baroque painter from Antwerp also accepted modest commissions, such as designing the book illustrations and the printer's mark for the *Officina Plantiniana*. Sometimes he used pen and paper for this, and sometimes he made a sketch in oil on panel. Between 1618 and 1629, Jan van Meurs was the business partner of Balthasar I Moretus. His printer's mark depicts a hen sitting on her eggs, along with the motto 'Noctu incubando diuque'. The head of Minerva and the owl symbolise night-time, and the head of Mercury and the cockerel daytime. The antique oil lamp symbolises the light disseminated by the press, and the caduceus and trumpet refer to commerce and fame.

Peter Paul Rubens,
Design for the printer's mark of Jan van Meurs,
after 1618.

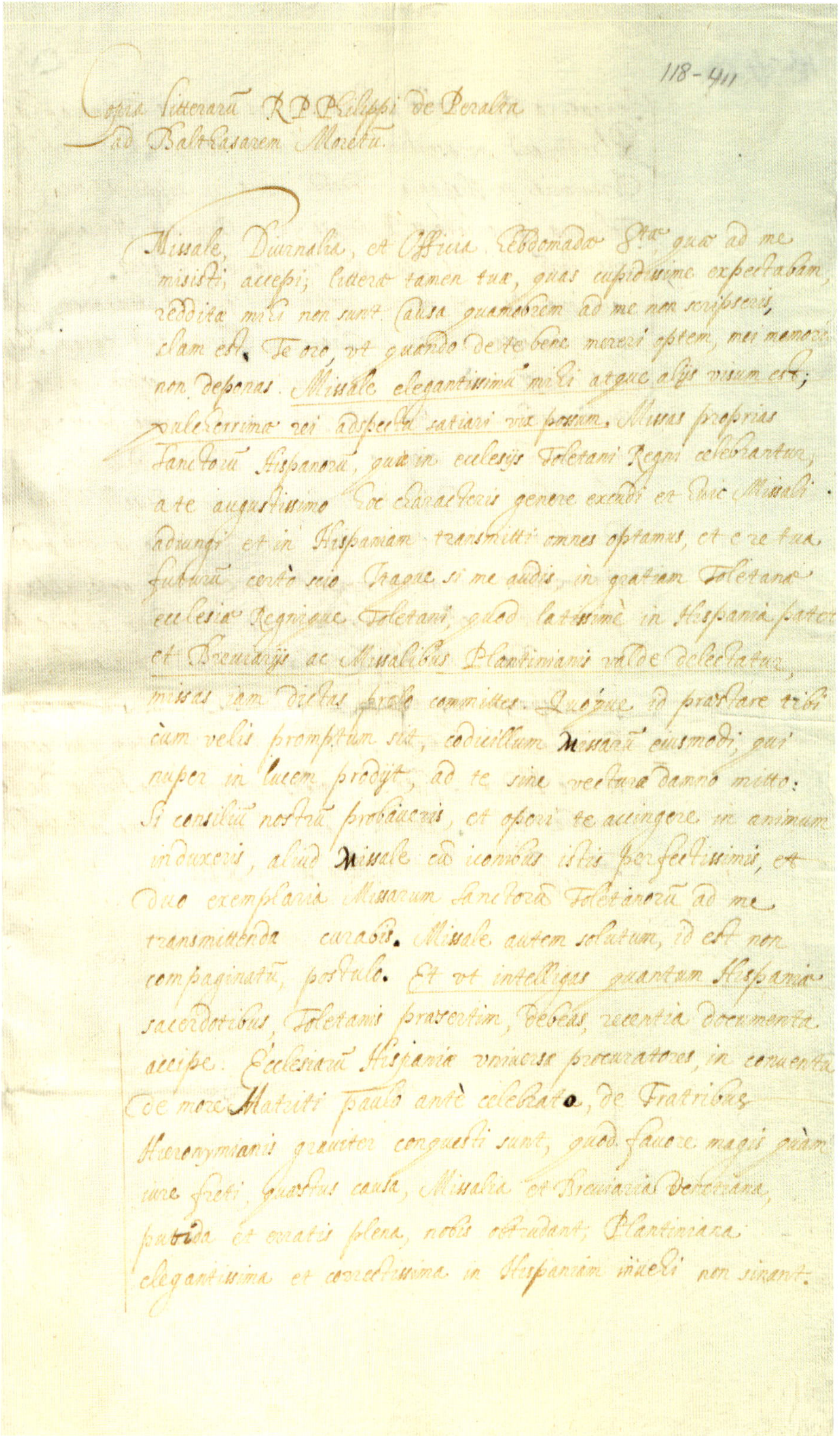

118-411

Copia litterarũ R.P. Philippi de Peralta
ad Balthasarem Moretũ.

Missale, Diurnalia, et Officia Hebdomadæ S.tæ quæ ad me misisti; accepi; litteræ tamen tuæ, quas cupidissime expectabam, redditæ mihi non sunt. Causa quamobrem ad me non scripseris, clam est. Te oro, vt quando de te bene mereri optem, mei memoriam non deponas. Missale elegantissimũ mihi atque alijs visum est; pulcherrimæ rei adspectu satiari vix possum. Missas proprias Sanctorũ Hispanorũ, quæ in ecclesijs Toletani Regni celebrantur, a te augustissimo hoc characteris genere excudi et huic Missali adiungi et in Hispaniam transmitti omnes optamus, et e re tua futurũ certò scio. Itaque si me audis, in gratiam Toletanæ ecclesiæ Regnique Toletani, quod latissimè in Hispania patet et Breuiarijs ac Missalibus Plantinianis valde delectatur, missas iam dictas prelo committes. Quòque id præstare tibi cùm velis promptum sit, codicillum Missarũ eiusmodi, qui nuper in lucem prodijt, ad te sine vecturæ damno mitto. Si consiliũ nostrũ probaueris, et operi te accingere in animum induxeris, aliud Missale cũ iconibus istis perfectissimis, et duo exemplaria Missarum Sanctorũ Toletanorũ ad me transmittenda curabis. Missale autem solutum, id est non compaginatũ, postulo. Et vt intelligas quantum Hispaniæ sacerdotibus, Toletanis præsertim, debeas, recentia documenta accipe. Ecclesiarũ Hispaniæ vniuersæ procuratores, in conuentu de more Matriti paulò antè celebrato, de Fratribus Hieronymianis grauiter conquesti sunt, quod fauore magis quàm iure freti, quæstus causa, Missalia et Breuiaria Venetiana, putrida et erratis plena, nobis obtrudant; Plantiniana elegantissima et correctissima in Hispaniam inuehi non sinant.

Letter from Philippus de Peralta to Jan II and Balthasar I Moretus, 15 October 1613.

woodcuts or engravings is fairly simple. The copies illustrated with woodcuts were first printed on the relief printing press with the woodcut blocks together with the text. When enough copies had been printed, the woodcut blocks were removed and replaced by spacers so that the space for the illustrations was left empty. These last sheets then went to a workshop with an intaglio press to print the engravings in the right place.

This division between woodcuts and engravings was used for liturgical works such as the missal and the breviary and the *Officium beatae Mariae Virginis*. It was also used for other prayer books such as the *Officium hebdomadae sanctae*, the *Diurnale Romanum* and popular prayer books like Petrus Canisius' *Manuale catholicorum* (and its Dutch and French translations) and Henricus Costerius' *Modus orandi*. The difference in price between the two versions could be quite substantial. A copy illustrated with engravings often cost twice that of one with woodcuts.

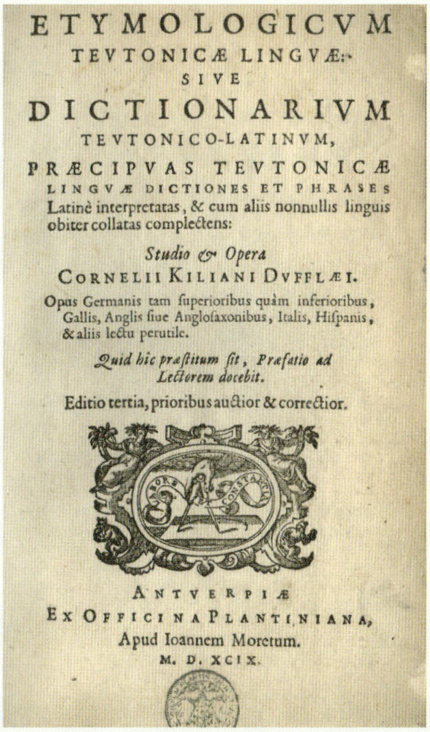
ETYMOLOGICVM
TEVTONICÆ LINGVÆ:
SIVE
DICTIONARIVM
TEVTONICO-LATINVM,
PRÆCIPVAS TEVTONICÆ
LINGVÆ DICTIONES ET PHRASES
Latinè interpretatas, & cum aliis nonnullis linguis obiter collatas complectens:
Studio & Opera
CORNELII KILIANI DVFFLÆI.
Opus Germanis tam ſuperioribus quàm inferioribus, Gallis, Anglis ſiue Angloſaxonibus, Italis, Hiſpanis, & aliis lectu perutile.
Quid hic præſtitum ſit, Præfatio ad Lectorem docebit.
Editio tertia, prioribus auctior & correctior.
ANTVERPIÆ
EX OFFICINA PLANTINIANA,
Apud Ioannem Moretum.
M. D. XCIX.

Plantin had a great interest in dictionaries. As a foreigner, he tried to learn Dutch as quickly as possible. Not being able to find a good dictionary, he started to compile his own. Due to lack of time, however, he called on experts to finish his work, one of whom was his regular proofreader Cornelis Kiliaan. Words grew to become his passion. Published in 1599, Kiliaan's *Etymologicum teutonicae linguae* was the very first explanatory dictionary of the Dutch language. He regarded the Brabant dialect as being 'true' Dutch.
He did not restrict himself to merely listing existing Dutch words, but also explained their meanings, partly by comparing them to words from other languages. Kiliaan was the first person in Europe to really bring language comparison into practice.

On several occasions Plantin printed books of hours with illustrations which were placed in a frame. He could then vary the woodcuts and engravings in three combinations: engraved illustrations and frames, engraved illustrations and woodcut frames, and both illustrations and frames in woodcut. Each variant had its own price and targeted a specific class of customer.

In Plantin's time the copies illustrated with woodcuts led the field by a clear margin. In the course of the first half of the seventeenth century the prevalence of copies illustrated with woodcuts gradually declined in favour of copies illustrated with engravings and by 1650 copies illustrated with engravings were printed almost to the exclusion of woodcuts. By then woodcuts served

Lodovico Guicciardini, *Description de touts les Pais-Bas*, Christophe Plantin, 1582. Guicciardini describes the economy, politics, language, flora, fauna and national character of the thriving Netherlands. The book was published more than sixty times by various printers. The author pays a great deal of attention to Antwerp, his home city. He also describes the devastating influence of the Spanish War on the prosperous country.

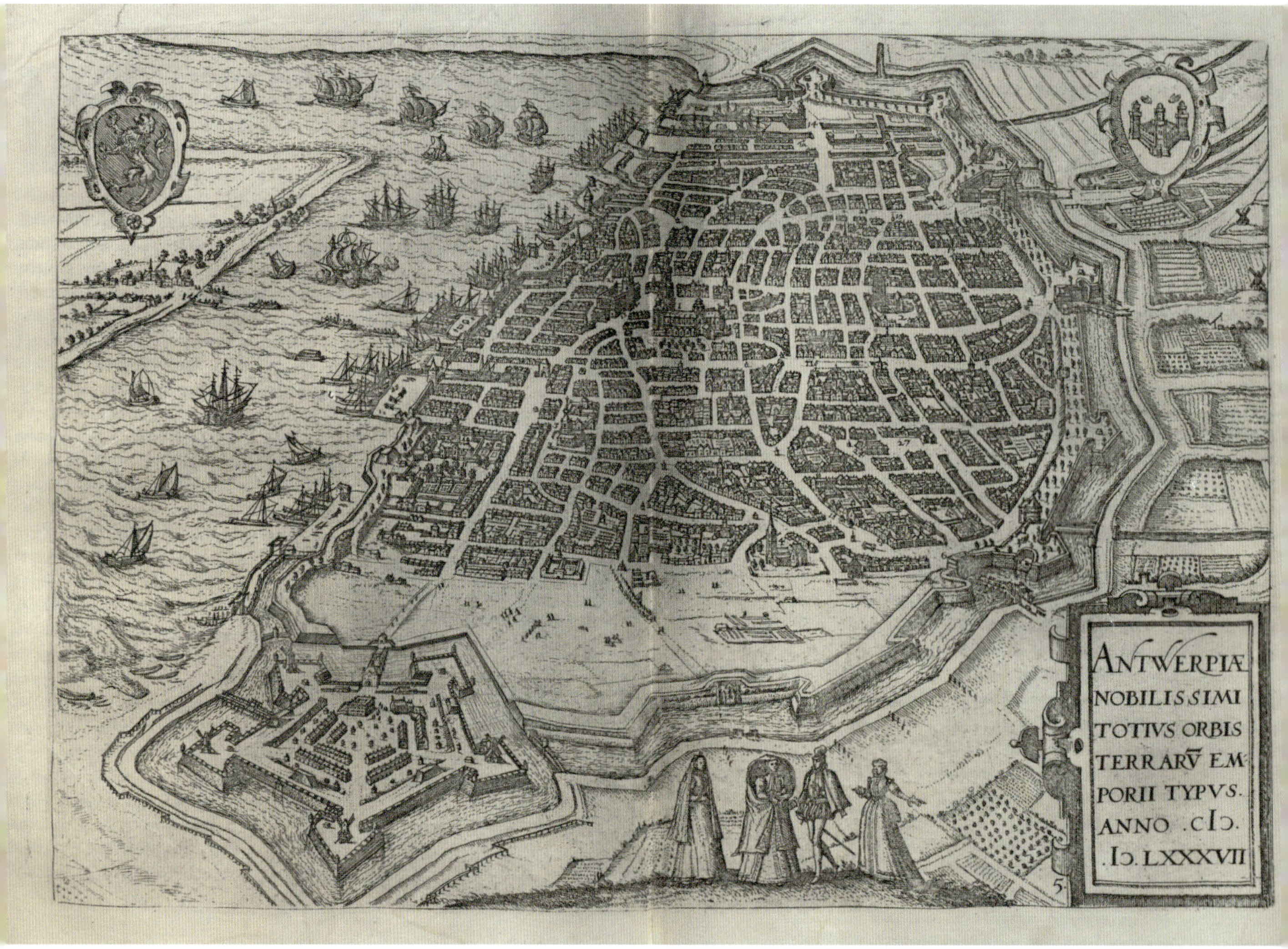

Richard Stanihurst, *Hebdomada Mariana*, Jan I Moretus, 1609, pp. 68–69, showing Our Lady of Assumption. Above, a copy with woodcuts, and below one with copper engravings.

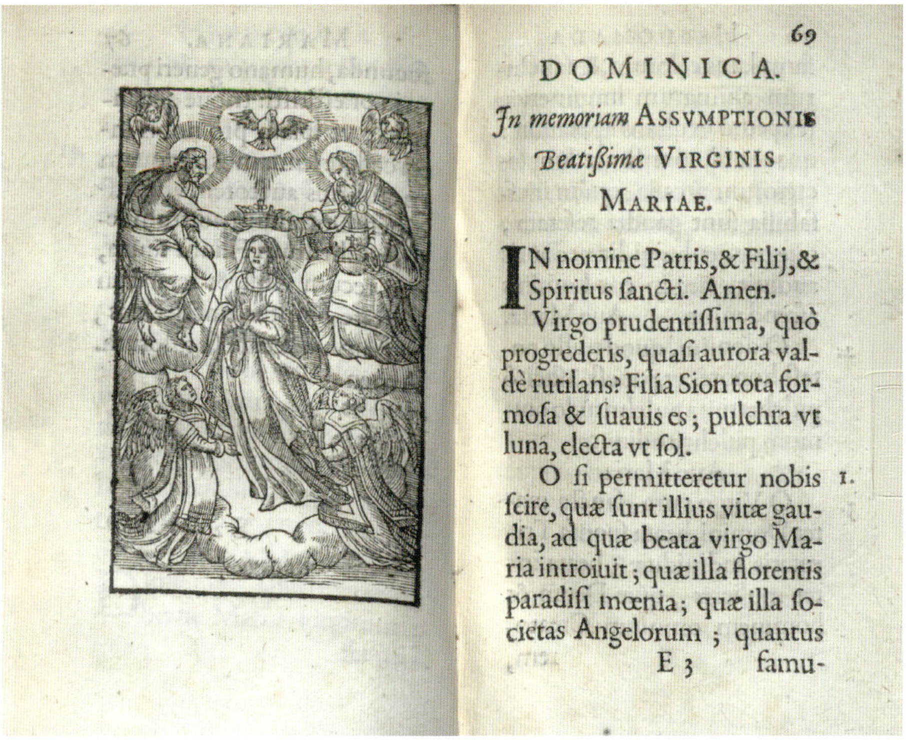

69

DOMINICA.

In memoriam ASSVMPTIONIS *Beatißimæ* VIRGINIS MARIAE.

IN nomine Patris,& Filij,& Spiritus ſancti. Amen.

Virgo prudentiſſima, quò progrederis, quaſi aurora valdè rutilans? Filia Sion tota formoſa & ſuauis es; pulchra vt luna, electa vt ſol.

O ſi permitteretur nobis 1.
ſcire, quæ ſunt illius vitæ gau-
dia, ad quæ beata virgo Ma-
ria introiuit; quæ illa florentis
paradiſi mœnia; quæ illa ſo-
cietas Angelorum ; quantus

E 3 famu-

69

DOMINICA.

In memoriam ASSVMPTIONIS *Beatißimæ* VIRGINIS MARIAE.

IN nomine Patris,& Filij,& Spiritus ſancti. Amen.

Virgo prudentiſſima, quò progrederis, quaſi aurora valdè rutilans? Filia Sion tota formoſa & ſuauis es; pulchra vt luna, electa vt ſol.

O ſi permitteretur nobis 1.
ſcire, quæ ſunt illius vitæ gau-
dia, ad quæ beata virgo Ma-
ria introiuit; quæ illa florentis
paradiſi mœnia; quæ illa ſo-
cietas Angelorum ; quantus

E 3 famu-

Woodcut of the joint printers' mark of Plantin, Nutius and Steelsius.

only to illustrate small-format liturgical works or works destined for the German market.

Moretus extended the practice of illustrating a part of the print run with woodcuts and a part with engravings (or etchings) to the printer's mark or vignette on the title page, albeit on a smaller scale. While a woodcut printer's mark or vignette was placed in most of the copies in a print run, an engraved printer's mark or vignette was placed in a relatively small number of copies. The copies with an engraved printer's mark were slightly more expensive, partly because they were usually printed on more expensive paper. Long gone were the 1550s when Plantin's business consisted mainly of reprinting small, popular works in French and often for other publishers. Or so it seemed, for he still often worked with other publishers. First and foremost there were the publications he printed on behalf of other publishers and, conversely, in the 1570s when he was suddenly inundated with work on the *Biblia regia* and the commissions for liturgical works for Spain, he paid other printers to print for him. Apart from these cases, he also published several editions in a proper joint venture with other publishers. A good example of this is the handbook of ecclesiastical law, the *Corpus iuris canonici*, which he published in 1573 with Joannes Steelsius' heirs and with Philippus Nutius. For this publication the Mechelen artist Peeter vander Borcht designed a special printer's mark that combined the marks of the three publishing houses. With the Cologne publisher Arnold Mylius, Plantin published voluminous editions in folio, such as the works of the church father Hieronymus in eight parts (1579) and the *Synonymia geographica* by the cartographer Abraham Ortelius (1578). Each shouldered a share of the investment costs and then divided the copies between them. In particular Plantin often worked with the Antwerp printmaker and dealer Filips Galle. Plantin regularly printed texts for Galle's series of prints, printed and sold Galle's publications of Ortelius' pocket atlas in the different languages and also together with him published an illustrated catechism

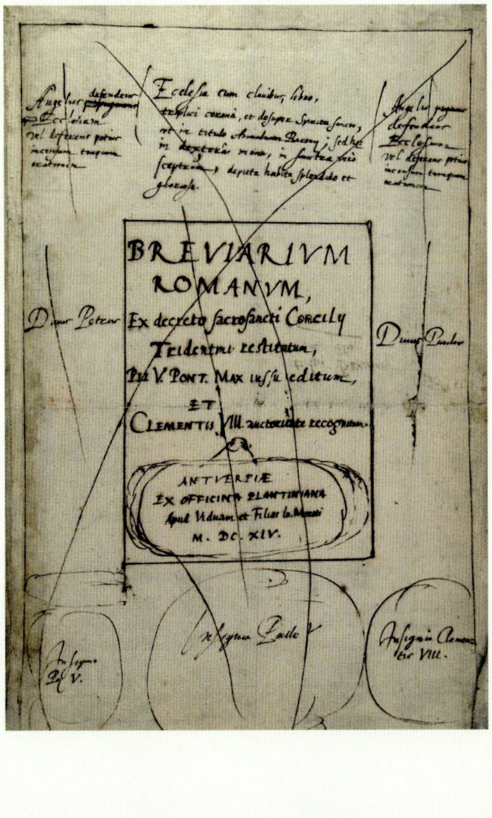

The goal of every good publisher is innovation. Balthasar I Moretus invited Peter Paul Rubens to join him in developing a new book: a Baroque edition with high-quality illustrations that became a true showpiece. In the seventeenth century, the job of layout designer did not exist as yet. Balthasar I took it upon himself to make sketches, in order to show Rubens how he envisaged his new book. Rubens then set to work on the basis of these instructions.

Balthasar I Moretus, *Initial sketch of the title page of the Breviarium Romanum*, 1614.

La magnifique, et sumptueuse pompe funebre ... du ... Charles cinquieme, Christophe Plantin and Hieronymus Cock, 1559. This album was Plantin's first big work, with which he established his fame as a publisher, even though he printed only the short text. The twelve-metre-long procession reads like a comic strip. The funeral band goes

by the Jesuit Peter Canisius (*Institutiones christianae, seu parvus catechismus*, 1589), each shouldering half the cost of the print run.

Unlike his father-in-law, Jan Moretus was far less inclined to collaborate with other publishers and printers. At first Jan Moretus rejected a deal proposed by Arnold Mylius for the publication of the popular collection of sermons by Thomas Stapleton. Just as he didn't want other publishers to print his editions, he didn't print those of others, he wrote. It took all Mylius' powers of persuasion to come to an arrangement with him. The book was printed at Mylius' expense, but Moretus' name appeared on the title page. Only with Theodore Galle (and a few other print dealers) did Jan Moretus work closely and on a regular basis. In 1598 Theodore Galle, Filips Galle's successor,

from left to right, with the coffin of Charles V, dignitaries, musicians, standard-bearers and the ship with the virtues Faith, Hope and Love. Son Philip II brings up the rear of the procession. The work was sold in the form of a roll or book, in the five languages of Charles' empire: Dutch, French, German, Spanish and Italian.

married Moretus' daughter Catherine. The Moretus-Galle cooperation is the one that springs to mind in the case of the illustrated works of the Jesuit Joannes David. Both publishers contributed to these editions: the Galle workshop took care of the illustrations (sometimes a hundred engravings for one edition) and also partially sold them, while the *Officina Plantiniana* printed the texts which they also partly sold separately. At the same time they sold each other the printed texts and illustrations. So both publishers retained their independence and ensured that they could also sell the parts of these editions separately. It was a win-win situation for both.

Because of the choice of subject matter and the large number of religious and humanist works, many of the editions produced by the Plantin publishing house were in Latin. However, in general in the course of the sixteenth century the number of publications in modern languages increased to the detriment of Latin. While in the fifteenth century editions in Latin had accounted for more than 75% of the whole book production, this share fell in the sixteenth century and by the end of the century perhaps more than half of the works appeared in the vernacular. The *Officina Plantiniana* did not go along with this general trend. Plantin wrote that he preferred to leave works in Dutch to other Antwerp publishers. In his letter of 20 September 1586 to Christophorus Vladeraccus, a teacher in Den Bosch, he wrote that he preferred not to publish books in Dutch to avoid the jealousy of printers of the vernacular unless they had previously turned down the publication and unless he thought that the work in question would be of value to the Christian community. Under Plantin, editions in French followed in second place after Latin but under his successors Dutch ousted French from second place. Latin was still unquestionably the front-runner. Under Balthasar II Moretus the number of works in Latin even topped 85% because of

Joannes David, *Veridicus christianus*, Jan I Moretus, 1601.

For almost two centuries, the Plantin printing house published the laws of Antwerp, which regulated everyday goings on in the city. They give us a good idea of what life was like at the time. On 9 January 1597, the city council took measures against the Black Death, or the plague.
There was a temporary ban on commerce on Vrijdagmarkt, 'As the Black Death (God help us) is spreading all over the city, especially in the vicinity of IJzeren Waag and Vrijdagmarkt, through dirty old clothes and household items from infected places... the city decrees that in the coming two months nobody may sell old clothes, furniture or household items at Luizenmarkt or Vrijdagmarkt...' Signed G. Kieffel.

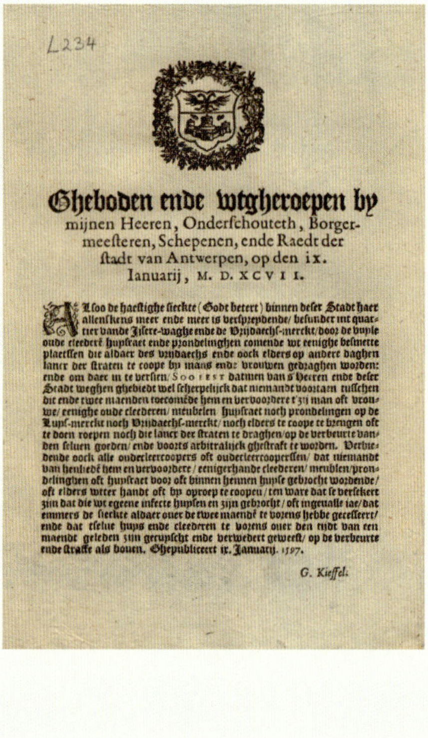

L234

GhebODen ende wtgheroepen by mijnen Heeren, Onderschouteth, Borgermeesteren, Schepenen, ende Raedt der stadt van Antwerpen, op den ix. Ianuarij, M. D. XCVII.

Alsoo de haestighe sieckte (Godt betert) binnen deser Stadt haer allenskens meer ende meer is verspreydende/ besunder int quartier vande Ijsere-waghe ende de Vrydaechs-merckt/ door de vuyle oude cleederẽ huysraet ende prondelinghen comende wt eenighe besmette plaetssen die aldaer des vrydaechs ende oock elders op andere daghen lanck der straten te coope by mans ende vrouwen gedraghen worden: ende om daer in te versien/ Soo eest datmen van s'Heeren ende deser Stadt weghen ghebiedt wel scherpelijck dat niemandt voortaen tusschen dit ende twee maenden toecomẽde hem en vervoordere t'zij man oft vrouwe/ eenighe oude cleederen/ meubelen huysraet noch prondelingen op de Luys-merckt noch Vrydaechs-merckt/ noch elders te coope te brengen oft te doen roepen noch die lanck der straten te draghen/ op de verbeurte vanden seluen goeden/ ende voorts arbitralijck ghestraft te worden. Verbiedende oock alle oudecleercoopers oft oudecleercooperssen/ dat niemandt van henliedẽ hem en vervoordere/ eenigerhande cleederen/ meublen/ prondelinghen oft huysraet voor oft binnen hennen huyse gebrocht wordende/ oft elders wtter handt oft by oproep te coopen/ ten ware dat se verseker zijn dat die wt egeene infecte huysen en zijn gebrocht/ oft ingevalle iae/ dat emmers de sieckte aldaer over de twee maendẽ te voorens hebbe gecesseert/ ende dat tselue huys ende cleederen te voorens over den tijdt van een maendt geleden zijn geruyscht ende verwedert geweest/ op de verbeurte ende straffe als boven. Ghepubliceert ix. Ianuarij. 1597.

G. Kieffel.

IHS
VERIDICVS
CHRISTIANVS.
Auctore P. IOANNE DAVID,
Sacerdote Societatis IESV.
AVDITE ME
Venite filij
Ventura interrogate me. Isa. 45.
ANTVERPIÆ
Ex officina Plantiniana,
CIↃ. IↃCI.

לא ימוש ספר התורה הזה מפיך והגית בו יומם ולילה למען תשמור לעשות ככל הכתוב בו כי אז תצליח את דרכך ואז תשכיל:

כל ארחות יי' חסד ואמת

חמשה חומשי תורה

נדפס עם רב העיון על ידי כריס'טופורו
פלנ"טין במצות השר בומב"ירגי
יצ"ו בשנת שכ"ו לפ"ק פה
העיר המהוללה

אנוי"רשה

Biblia Hebraea, Christophe Plantin, 1566: title page.

Joannes Valverde, *Vivae imagines partium corporis humani*, Christophe Plantin, 1566 Valverde copied Vesalius' *De humani corporis fabrica*. Plantin reprinted the book by Valverde. It was Plantin's first book with copper plates. His main aim was to show that he could deliver higher quality.

the dominance of liturgical editions. Several works were produced in Spanish and Italian, but their number was very limited; not a single German or English edition was published at the Officina.

For his Bible editions and in particular the publication of the *Biblia regia* Plantin had invested heavily in Hebrew typefaces. He used them to print a large number of Hebrew bibles and grammar books which were sold to Jewish communities and Christian theologians wishing to read the Old Testament in the original Hebrew. After Plantin's death in 1589 most of the Hebrew types ended up in Leiden. Franciscus I Raphelengius, who held the Hebrew chair at the University of Leiden, specialized in Hebrew publications and laid the foundations for the development of Hebrew typography in the Dutch republic. In Antwerp, on the other hand, the Moretuses now only printed the occasional text in Hebrew.

From the second half of the seventeenth century the Plantin publishing house specialized in liturgical works and bibles almost

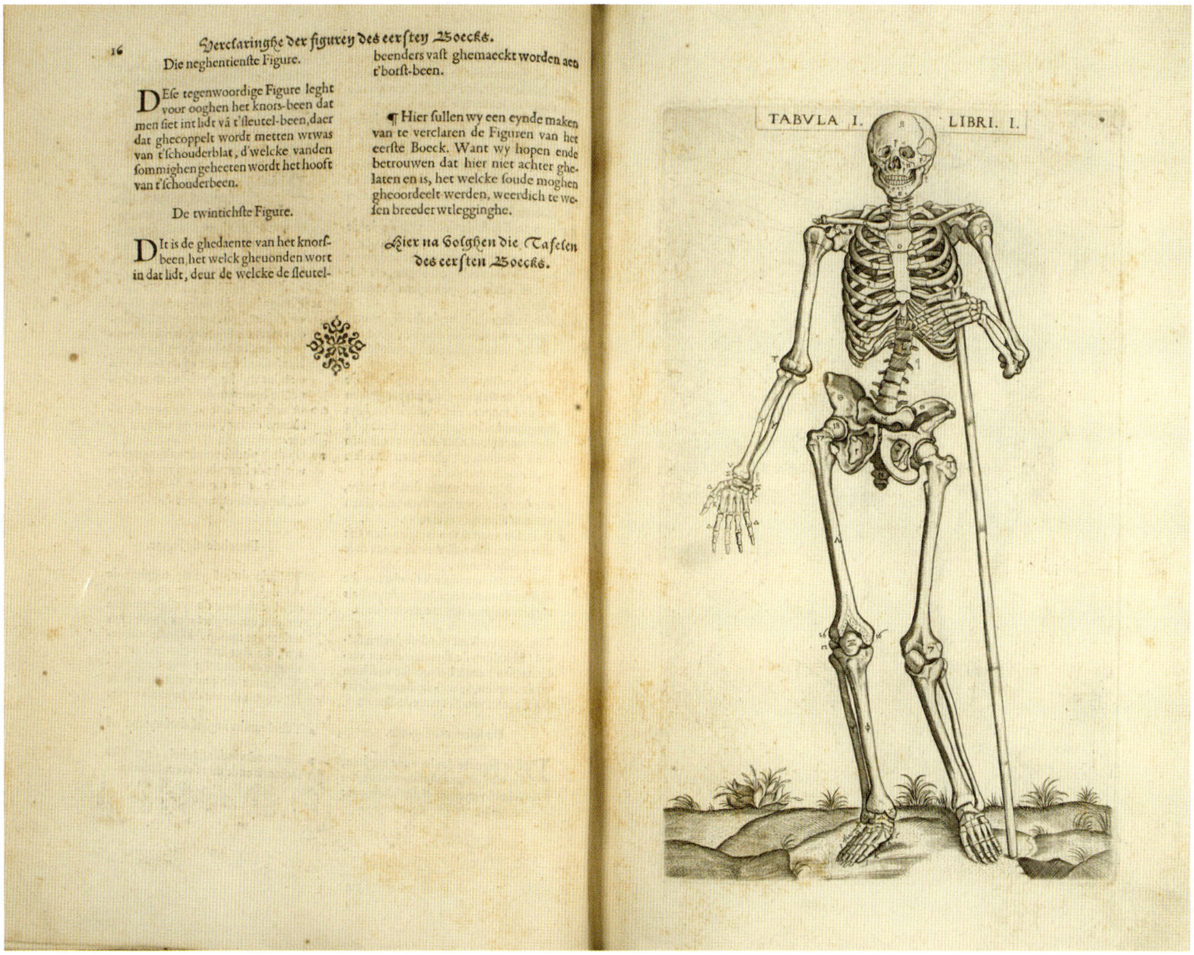

to the exclusion of other printed work. This change came about on Balthasar II Moretus' watch. In the 1640s the percentage of religious and liturgical works out of the total number of editions accounted for 70% and 50% respectively; that figure rose to 100% and 92% in the 1670s. Balthasar II Moretus was ignoring the advice given to him on the death of Balthasar I in 1641 by his cousin Franciscus II Raphelengius, at the time an experienced, seventy-year-old Leiden publisher. He urged Balthasar II Moretus to go on printing liturgical works because of the profitability of these editions, but also to publish other works because that would enhance the publishing house's reputation. 'Experience teaches', he wrote, 'that the black and red books or liturgical editions are more profitable. But because they are nearly always the same works and in the same formats and because most have the same titles, they usually benefit the financial side of the business more than the reputation of the publishing house that produces them. So it is important to intersperse books of the liturgy with other editions. To safeguard your reputation, while the books which are less lucrative do not ruin you, you can limit the number of presses intended for the non-liturgical works, but not do away with them entirely'.

Balthasar III, the son and successor of Balthasar II Moretus, took over from his father in 1674. The *Officina Plantiniana* now concentrated on printing liturgical works for Spain; other works were printed only by way of exception. Not only did Balthasar III end the production of all the non-liturgical works, but he also ceased to trade in all the other books which

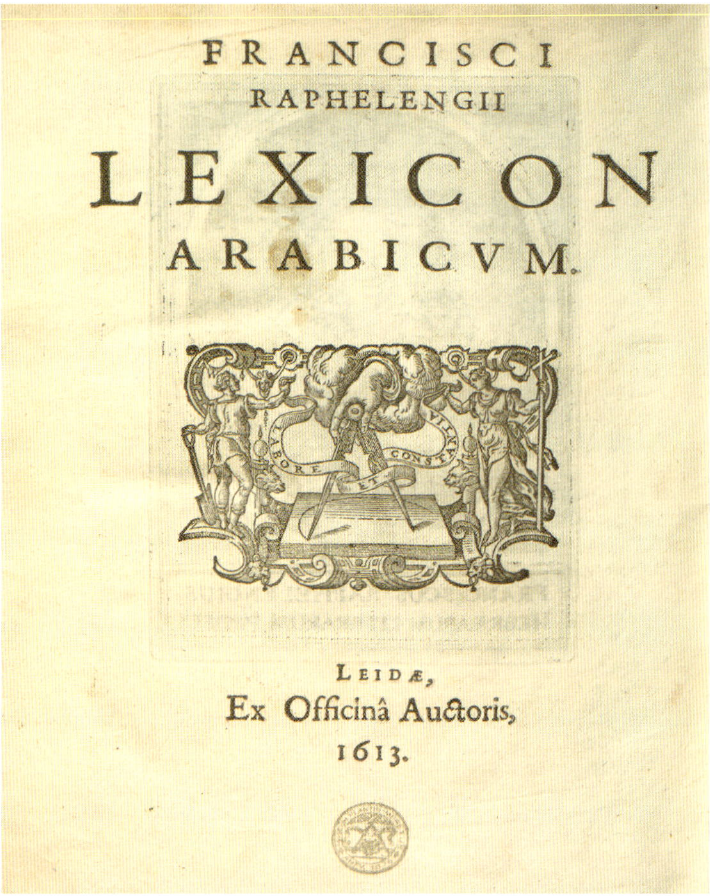

FRANCISCI
RAPHELENGII
LEXICON
ARABICVM.

LEIDÆ,
Ex Officinâ Auctoris,
1613.

Franciscus I Raphelengius, *Lexicon Arabicum*, Franciscus Raphelengius, Leiden, 1613. During his studies, Raphelengius discovered that there was no Arabic dictionary, so he compiled his own.

Lucas Jansz. Waghenaer, *Teerste deel vande spieghel der zeevaerdt*, Leiden, Christophe Plantin, 1584. Plantin's maritime atlases are the finest of the sixteenth century. They form a milestone in the development of maritime cartography.

Ghedruct tot Leyden/ by Christoffel Plantijn/

voor Lucas Janssz/ Waghenaer van Enckhuysen.

Anno M. D. LXXXIIII.

327

Op den vierten dagh inde maent februarij van desen te-
ghenwoordighen Jaere Sesthien hondert en seven-
en seventigh bekenne ick francois foppens ghecocht te
hebben, ende te coopen mits desen van Juffrou de Wedu-
we vande Heer Baltasar Moretus Eene Masse van-
de Sorteringe van hare swerte Boecken, Libri negri ghe-
noemt, bestaende in

390. Lipsij opera fol. 4 Vol.
290 — in Senecam folio.
1380 — in Tacitum folio.
170 Goltzij opera fol. 5 Vol
453. — Icones Imperatorū fol.
150 — Graecia. fol.
100 Biblia Mariana et Sa fol. 2 V.
400. Harej Annales fol. 2 Vol.
750 Palavicini Historia Conc. Trident. 4° 3 Vol
455. Corderius in Psalmos fol. 3 Vol
222. — Tomus 2us separatim.
151 — Job. folio.
222. — in Lucam fol.
41 — et Possinus in Matthaeum fol. 2 V.
100 Rubenius de re Vestiaria 4°
600. Nierembergius de adoratione 8°

Voor alle de welcke hier beschreven en ghespecificeerde
Boecken ick verclaere aende Voorseyde Juffrou Weduwe
schuldigh te wesen, en belove en verobligere my voor de
selve te betalen binnen Antwerpen aen haer
aen hare erfgenamen ofte aen haere actie heb-
bende de Somme van Drie dusent ende Vyf-
hondert Ponden Vlaems eens in goeden ganck-
baeren Wissel-gelde, ende dat in den tyde ende
Termyn van Seven Jaeren, het een Jaer het

vaste.

were still in stock. In the 1670s thousands of copies of his father's and grandfather's impressive publications were sold in large numbers to the Brussels bookseller Francois Foppens and to the Verdussens in Antwerp.

That degree of specialization has its risks. Around 1675 the Hieronymites of San Lorenzo, the monastic order in Spain responsible for the sale and distribution of the liturgical works, ran into financial difficulty and could no longer pay its bills. The cause, they claimed, was the high prices the *Officina Plantiniana* charged for printed work. Balthasar III was left with little choice other than to head for Spain and open up negotiations. After all, there were plenty of competitors ready to fill his shoes, including the firm Anisson in Lyon which printed cheap liturgical editions, even with the imprint of the *Officina Plantiniana* on the title page. Things turned out well for Balthasar III Moretus. On 12 July 1680 a formal contract was ceremoniously celebrated in the monastery of San Lorenzo. The trade with Spain had been salvaged and Balthasar III could return to Antwerp with an easy mind.

After 1705 the Plantin publishing house only printed liturgical works. In the period 1716–1730 Joannes Jacobus Moretus sent books worth 1,097.040 guilders to Madrid and Seville, a gigantic sum at the time. After a brief drop in production as a result of the Austrian War of Succession (1740–1748), there were still eight printing presses in operation on the death of Joannes Jacobus.

However, in the second half of the eighteenth century activity at the *Officina Plantiniana* began its downward spiral. The main reason for this was the termination of exports of liturgical works to Spain. On 15 April 1764 King Carlos III of Spain confirmed an agreement between the Hieronymites and the newly-founded *Compania de Impresores y libreros de Madrid* for printing liturgical works. He then withdrew all privileges from foreign printers who supplied Spain with liturgical works. Not even works which had already been printed could be exported to Spain. This time there could be no negotiations as in Balthasar III Moretus' day at the end of the seventeenth century. The number of printing presses in the company was reduced to three. From then on the *Officina Plantiniana* was dependent on the local market in the Austrian Netherlands.

In 1800 the Plantin printer's still had one book printer and one plate printer in its employ. Both were made redundant the following year. After a short period of activity from 1806 to 1808, in 1810 at the time of French rule, Frans Jozef Moretus informed the prefect of the *Departement des Deux Nèthes* that he was giving up printing, but that he was holding on to the tools of the trade in anticipation of better times. In 1828 Albert Moretus tried to start the printing business up again and took on six members of staff. To immortalize this fresh start in printing the employees wrote a poem in honour of Albert Moretus in which they described him as the 'hersteller der aloude en alom vermaerde Plantynsche artsdrukkery' (the restorer of the time-honoured and widely acclaimed Plantin printing house). Though things went well for a few years and new liturgical editions appeared from 1831, activity at the Plantin printing house gradually began

Contract dated 4 February 1677 between Balthasar III Moretus and François Foppens for the sale of hundreds of copies of earlier editions from the Plantin printing house.

to wane. When Edward Moretus, Albert's younger brother, inherited the *Officina Plantiniana* in 1865, he also attempted to inject new life into the business, but it was short-lived. The year of publication 1866 appears inside the last dated printed work, a prayer book entitled *Horae diurnae propriae sanctorum trium ordinum S.P.N. Francisci*. Small printed matter may have been produced in 1867.

Both Albert and Edward Moretus turned a blind eye to the new technologies. The first cast-iron hand press had appeared in 1797, while the first cylinder press which greatly speeded up the printing process saw the light of day in 1812. Moreover, both Albert and Edward Moretus continued to swear by the sort of books, liturgical works, that the *Officina Plantiniana* had printed for so many years and they made no attempt to innovate. In the meantime other publishers such as Hanicq in Mechelen had stepped into their shoes. The *Officina Plantiniana* finally had to concede defeat. Three hundred and eleven years separate the appearance of the first work printed by Plantin in 1555 and the last work printed by Edward Moretus, an achievement unmatched by any other printing house.

HORÆ
DIURNÆ
PROPRIÆ
SANCTORUM
TRIUM ORDINUM
S. P. N.
FRANCISCI,
A SS. DOMINO PIO PAPA VI.
DUDUM APPROBATÆ,
Una & cum officiis usque in præsens concessis auctæ.

ANTVERPIÆ,
EX ARCHYTYPOGRAPHIA PLANTINIANA.
M. D. CCC. LXVI.

Horae diurnae propriae sanctorum trium ordinum S.P.N. Francisci, Edward Moretus, 1866: title page.

Aen den weledelen heer, jonkheer Albertus Franciscus Hyacinthus Fredericus Moretus, hersteller der aloude en alom vermaerde Plantynsche artsdrukkery te Antwerpen, in het jaer 1828 (To Mr Albertus Franciscus Hyacinthus Fredericus Moretus Esquire, restorer of the time-honoured and renowned Plantin arch-printers, in Antwerp, in the year 1828), ode.

AEN DEN WELEDELEN HEER, JONKHEER

ALBERTUS FRANCISCUS HYACINTHUS FREDERICUS

MORETUS,

Hersteller der aloude en alom vermaerde

PLANTYNSCHE ARTSDRUKKERY

Te Antwerpen, in het jaer 1828.

EERDICHT.

TRIOMF! d'ARTSDRUKKERY gaet hier met roem herleéven;
Den Overwinnaer-tyd moet zich gevangen geéven:
Als nutten *arbeyd* met *volherding* is gepaerd,
Dan blyft den roem van 't werk, eeuw in eeuw uyt, vermaerd.
PLANTYN, doór *arbeyd*, konst, geleerdheyd, goede zeden,
Insteller van dit huys, gegrond op wyze reden,
Nam d'onderneéming aen met mannelyken moed,
En bragt z' in *vasten* staet, doór vroóm beleyd, met spoed....
De Drukzael dezes Mans, doór ouderdom vervallen,
Heéft in d'historie nog den grootsten naem van allen;
Philippus, spaenschen Vorst, haer noemt *Artsdrukkery*,
Dit koninglyk besluyt blyft haer gestadig by.
De boeken, daer gedrukt, in alle wereld-oórden
Verbreyden haeren glans en styven deze woórden;
Ja, haeren *arbeyd* praelt ten dienst' der Roomsche Kerk,
En haer' *volherding* blyft in 't geestelyke werk.
D'*Artsdrukkery* zal thans een' nieuwen luyster krygen,
Hoewel den stilstand haer kwam met de dood bedrygen:
Den *Passer*, naem van 't huys, nauwkeurigheyd bedied;
Het *tweekoleurig* juk de juystheyd steéds gebied.
Zy voórtyds zwanger was van allerschoonste vrugten
Zoo voór den Staet als Kerk; men ziet nog met genugten
Het vlaemsche Woórdenboek, gemaekt doór dien *Plantyn*,
Het geén', om d'aerdigheyd, nog wilt doórbladerd zyn;
Hy, franschman, voór die taek veél *arbeyd* moest besteéden,
En doór *volherding* was onz' taelkonst ingetreéden:
Na hem trad *Kiliaen van Duffel* in dit vak;
Hy toonde dat in hem den geest zyns meesters stak.
Den grooten *Lipsius*, berugt in alle landen,
Was aen *Plantyn* verknogt doór bryns en vriendschaps banden.
Kom, *Dodonæus*, kom, toon uwen *Kruydboek* thans;
Dit Pronkstuk, hoewel oud, bewaert den eerekrans,
Aen uwen *arbeyd* haest tweehonderd jaer gegeéven,
En met *volherding* nog tot heden blyft in 't leven;
Een wonder, aengehaeld om zyne zeldzaemheyd;
Men pryst geen oude boek op onz' verwaenden tyd....
Den aengetrouwden Zoőn, MORETUS nu geschreven,
Opvolger van *Plantyn*, heéft zyne konst verheven
Doór iver, smaek, verstand, met *arbeyd* vergezeld;
Joannes, als *Plantyn*, met agting word gemeld.
Van dan, *Moretus*-naem, geprent op duyzend werken,
Kwam zynen roem en glans vergrooten en versterken
Doór weêrde *Balthazars* en and're van dien stam,
Die 't vliegend peêrd der faem op zyne vleugels nam....
Maer d'ongestadigheyd der menschelyke zaeken
Deéd d'*oude Drukkery* ook haeren invloed smaeken;
Den *arbeyd* wierd gestaekt, de perssen stonden stil:
Volherding evenwel behield den ouden wil;
Den boekenhandel bleéf gestadiglyk voortdueren,
Dus Priester noch de Kerk moest deze ramp bezueren;
Er wierd, van tyd tot tyd, t'ontbrekend bygedrukt:
Maer dezen zwakken stand toch eyndelyk mislukt.
'T *Plantynsch* gebouw stort neér... De Drukkonst is aen 't treuren;
Het *rood en zwart* te niet! te niet die twee koleuren!....
Zwygt, Minnaers dezer konst, al schynt zy heden dood;
Er leéft een' weêrdig' Man, behulpzaem in den nood:
Den eélgeboren Heer, ALBERTUS, uytverkoren
Doór Gods voórzienigheyd, herstelt dat was verloren:
Hy voór de *Balthazars* noch voór *Joannes* zwigt
In iver tot die Konst; den Godsdienst hem verlicht.
Neén, geene lofspraek mag zyn' zedigheyd ontstigten;
Wat zou zy van dien Heer met waerheyd konnen dichten!
Maer onze borgery weét wat hy heéft gedaen,
En zyne mildheyd zal in 't g'heugen blyven staen....
Gy, Heer ALBERTUS, zult *Moretus*-naem doen gelden,
Met lof en vreugd zal m'hem in 't Catholykdom melden;
En 't *rood en zwart*, met eer, in kerk-latynsche tael,
Doór uw' *volherding* dus behoud den zegeprael.
Agtweêrden Heer, dat God U gunne zynen zegen,
Uw' onderneming kroon' met voórspoed uwer wegen,
En uwe Ziel vervoer', na *rooden-zwarten* Druk,
Waer geenen *arbeyd* is, maer *vastheyd* van geluk!

Met eerbied opgedraegen doór den Meester en de Gezellen dezer Drukkery.

The organisation of work at the *Officina Plantiniana*

KRISTOF SELLESLACH

The *Officina Plantiniana* was a well-oiled organisation. And it had to be, with sixty permanent employees, who sometimes got in each other's way on the shop floor. Who made sure that everything ran smoothly? How many men did it take to operate a printing press? What did the printers and compositors earn? How many hours a day did they work? The wage lists and the strict working regulations are kept in the archives, as are the employees' complaints books. The employees formed a sort of union, called the 'Kapel'.

INDEX SIVE SPECIMEN CHARACTERVM CHRISTOPHORI PLANTINI.

ANTVERPIÆ, M.D.LXVII.

Index Sive Specimen Characterum Christophori Plantini, in 4°, 1567
Catalogue showing the typefaces available at the Plantin printing house in 1567. It was probably compiled to convince Philip II that the *Officina Plantiniana* was capable of printing the Polyglot Bible.

IN 1574 – IN THE HEYDAY OF THE *Officina Plantiniana* – Christophe Plantin had sixteen printing presses in operation and employed sixty people. A further twenty or so craftsmen worked for him outside the printing house. These figures were extremely high for the time. In the same period, the renowned Estienne printing family in Geneva never had more than four printing presses in use. And in seventeenth century Paris, you could count the printing houses employing more than four people on one hand. The scale of Plantin's printing house was only equalled in the industrial revolution at the end of the eighteenth century. In such a large-scale business, of course, Christophe Plantin did not operate the presses himself. He led the company as 'Chief Executive Officer', and as the publisher with final responsibility, he decided which texts were published and which were not. For those he did publish, he determined the layout himself, in consultation with the author or client. As 'Chief Financial Officer', he collected the funds needed for ensuring the continuity of the presses.

Every tradesman had his own mark, which was used in dispatching goods. Christophe Plantin devised his own mark, 'PLNT', which is a contraction of all the consonants in the name 'Plantin'. The mark was put on all the barrels of books he sent to the Buchmesse book fair in Frankfurt, thus ensuring they would end up in his bookshop in Frankfurt.
The Moretuses continued to use the Plantin mark for dispatching books. Balthasar II Moretus also thought up a new way to use the trademark. From the mid-seventeenth century, he put it on the spines of the books in his library. His eldest son Balthasar III followed his example.

The pompous title 'arch-printer to the king' denoted an important job. On the order of the Spanish king Philip II, Christophe Plantin presented certificates to his fellow printers in the Netherlands. Only authorised printers were allowed to continue to practise their profession. Plantin carried out the king's orders very conscientiously.

On the certificate for his Antwerp colleague Jan Verwithagen, Plantin testified that Verwithagen 'appeared before me and [...] was found to be extremely skilled in all forms of the art of book printing, has a good understanding of Latin, Dutch and a little French, and is able to read and compose Greek'.

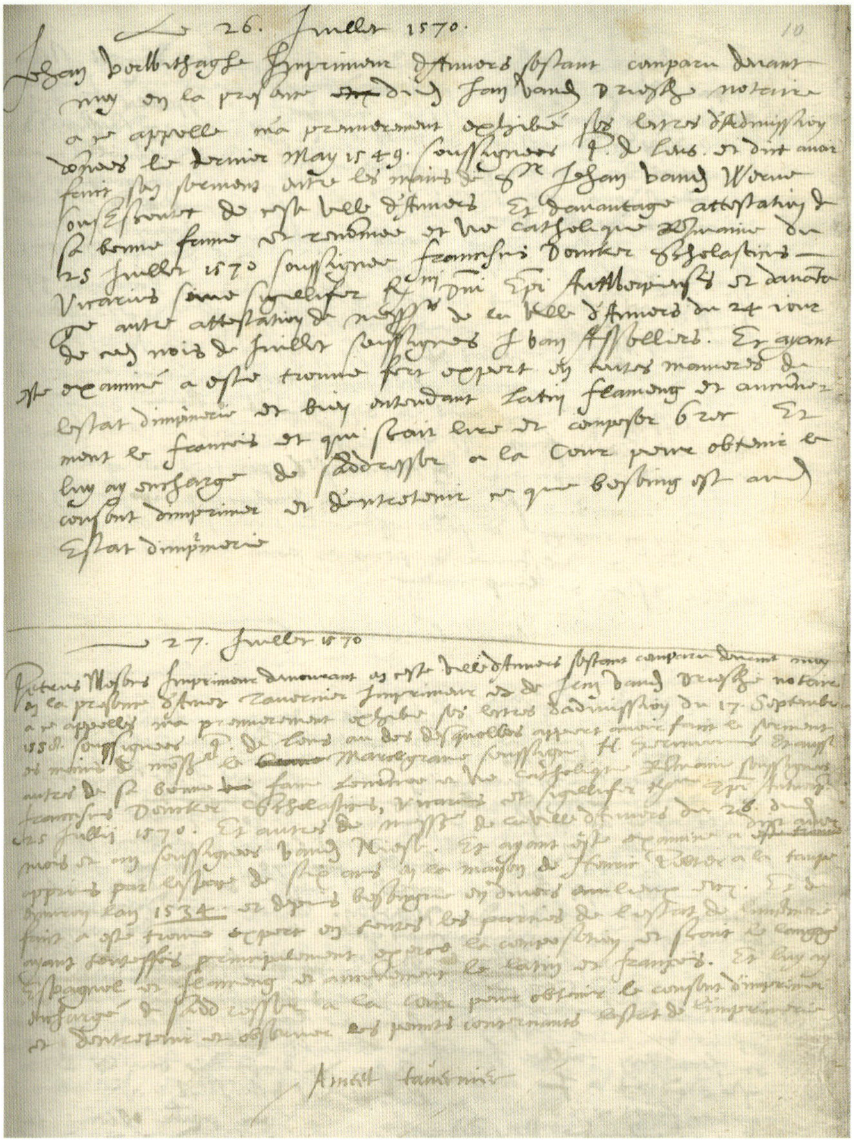
26. Juillet 1570.

27. Juillet 1570

In the type store, next to the printing room, the gouverneur was in charge of the type cases.

After printing, he also managed the sale of the printed books. And as 'Human Resources Manager', he led an extensive team, engaging and firing craftsmen. He set the wage policy and kept order on the shop floor. In short, the printer Christophe Plantin was a white-collar rather than a blue-collar worker. The ink stains on his hands came from administrative writing ink, and not from the printing presses themselves.

On the shop floor of the printing house, a variety of craftsmen worked together in coordination to produce the books. The *compositors* composed the text with separate lead letters. First, they set the text line by line on a setting stick. Complete lines were transferred to the galley (a tray with edges). When the page had been completely set, the compositors secured the type with string and then started on the next page. The matrix was the same size as the sheet of paper, so a matrix usually comprised several pages. The smaller the size of the book, the more pages the compositor could compose at the same time. Finally, the printed sheet of paper was folded and cut to the quires of the book. A book sometimes comprised hundreds of quires. A strange optical effect means that a print always shows a mirror image of the stamp. The compositors thus composed the type in reverse, which demanded a great deal of practice

PP. 104–105: The printing room with a row of five printing presses from the seventeenth and eighteenth century.

and concentration. Depending on the size of the book and that of the typeface, a compositor could set two to six matrices a week. As compositors were paid by matrix, a time-consuming matrix with many pages in a tiny typeface was paid better than an easy matrix with fewer pages in a large typeface. Compositors also earned more for a difficult Hebrew matrix. The average compositor earned about 8 stuivers a day. In Plantin's day, a litre of wheat cost 21 stuivers and a kilo of butter 60 stuivers. Two compositors were needed to keep one printing press running, although the ratio dropped for liturgical books – to four compositors for three presses. The two-colour missals required double the number of printing processes, as the red and black texts were printed separately. At the height of production in 1574, there were twenty compositors working at the Plantin printing house.

The *gouverneur* was in charge of the type cases in the case room. He lent the type cases to the compositors and inspected them on their return. As an experienced compositor, he was one of the highest earners among the compositors.

The *printers* formed the largest group of employees. Each press was operated by a team of two printers. One of them was responsible for inking the type evenly, while his mate carried out the actual printing. First he clamped the blank sheet of paper onto the moving part of the press and then he slid the sheet over the inked type. It took brute force to

Collection of *Grande musique* stamps. These music stamps were cut by Henri du Tour in 1577, on commission from Plantin.

The correctors' table in the proof-reading room.

push the handle. Finally, he removed the freshly printed sheet. This action took 15 to 20 seconds. An experienced team could repeat the action 2,500 times a day. Afterwards, a sheet was also printed on the reverse, so one press printed 1,250 sheets of paper a day on both sides. This figure, or a multiple of it, thus often corresponded to the print run of an edition. For liturgical books, the figure dropped to 500 sheets printed on both sides in red and black. When the print run was finished, the printers washed down the type with warm lye. The type was broken up and sorted back into the type cases. The actual printer, referred to in the sources as the 'premier', was responsible for the printing press. He had to arrive at the printing house earlier each day to prepare the press. The inker, or 'second', started an hour later, so earned half a stuiver less than the 'premier'. Printers earned slightly more than compositors, and were also paid for piece-work.

The *proofreaders* checked the type for errors. First, the printers made a proof of the type, and when it had been corrected they printed the whole run. Besides being fluent in Dutch and

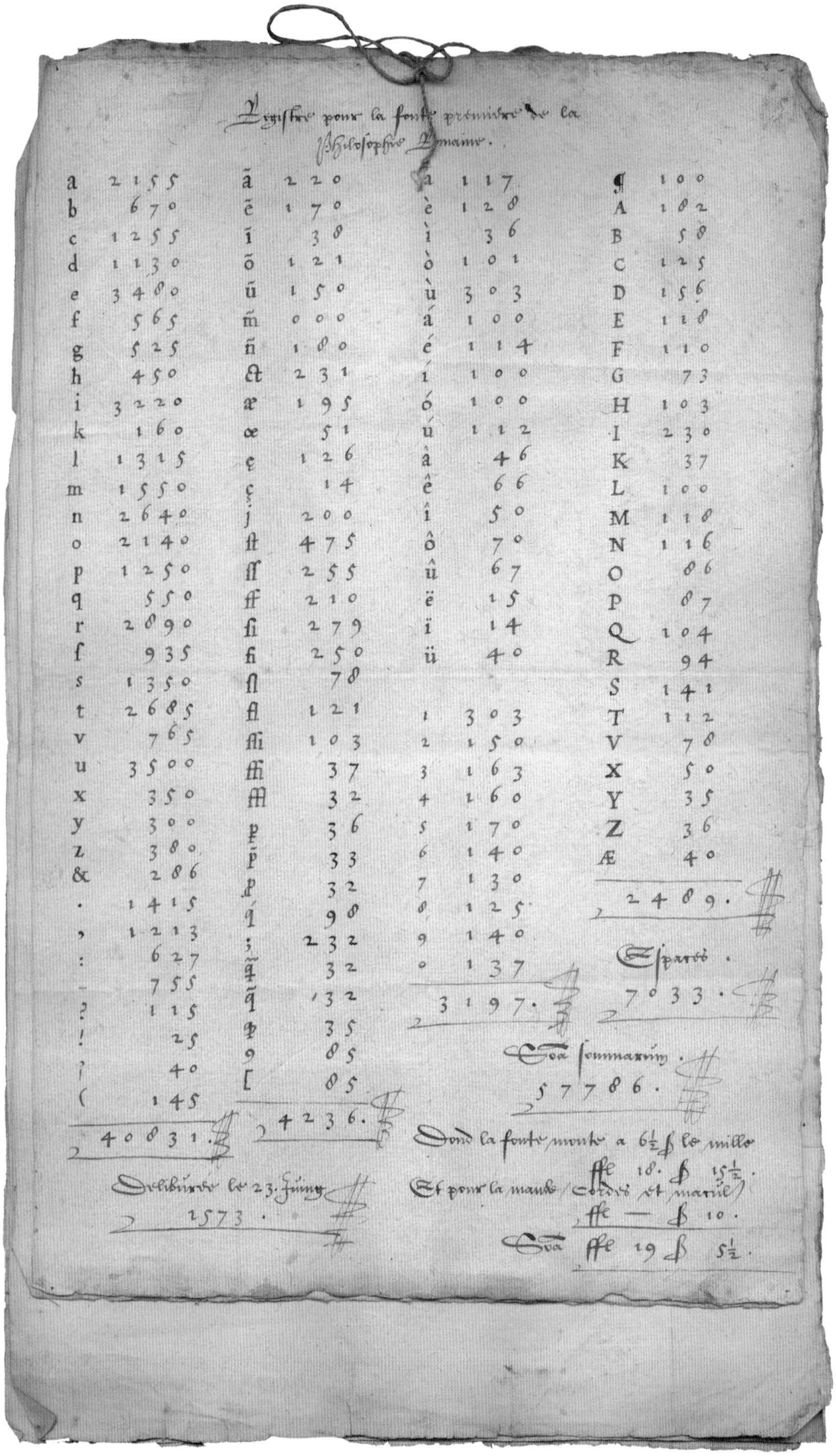
Registre pour la fonte premiere de la Philosophie Romaine.

a	2155	ã	220	à	117	¶	100
b	670	ẽ	170	è	120	A	182
c	1255	ĩ	38	ì	36	B	58
d	1130	õ	121	ò	101	C	125
e	3480	ũ	150	ù	303	D	156
f	565	m̃	000	á	100	E	118
g	525	ñ	180	é	114	F	110
h	450	ct	231	í	100	G	73
i	3220	æ	195	ó	100	H	103
k	160	œ	51	ú	112	I	230
l	1315	ę	126	â	46	K	37
m	1550	ç	14	ê	66	L	100
n	2640	j	200	î	50	M	118
o	2140	ſt	475	ô	70	N	116
p	1250	ſſ	255	û	67	O	86
q	550	ff	210	ë	15	P	87
r	2890	ſi	279	ï	14	Q	104
ſ	935	fi	250	ü	40	R	94
s	1350	ſl	78			S	141
t	2685	fl	121	1	303	T	112
v	765	ſſi	103	2	150	V	78
u	3500	ffi	37	3	163	X	50
x	350	ffl	32	4	160	Y	35
y	300	p̱	36	5	170	Z	36
z	380	p̄	33	6	140	Æ	40
&	286	ꝑ	32	7	130		2489.
.	1415	q̄	98	8	125		
,	1213	;	232	9	140		Esparés.
:	627	q̃	32	0	137		7033.
-	755	q̄	132		3197.		
?	115	ꝓ	35				
!	25	ꝯ	85				
;	40	[	85				
(	145						
	40831.		4236.				

Somme sommaire. 57786.

Dont la fonte monte a 6½ s le mille ₶ 18. s 15½.

Et pour la matiere (cordes et marine) ₶ — s 10.

Somme ₶ 19 s 5½.

Delivrée le 23. Juing 1573.

Invoice from Henri du Tour for the first casting of the *Philosophie romaine* font in 1573.

The typecasting room in the new wing, built by Balthasar I Moretus between 1620 and 1622.

French, proofreaders also had a good knowledge of Latin and Greek. Nevertheless, these white-collar workers earned considerably less than the blue-collar workers, like the printers and compositors. In Plantin's day, a proofreader worked on two to three presses.

The *gatherers* had the lowest status on the shop floor. They folded the printed sheets into quires and sorted the quires in the correct order of the book, turning piles of identical printed sheets into piles of unbound books. Gatherers were also used as errand boys for all sort of additional jobs. Gatherers earned only half as much as printers.

There were no *type founders* working in the *Officina* in Plantin's day. The lead type was founded on the basis of copper matrices elsewhere. For example, the type cutter Hendrik van den Keere, from Ghent, founded the lead type on the basis of stamps he had designed himself. In 1622, Plantin's grandson Balthasar Moretus had a type foundry installed in the new wing, which was in use until 1660, and again in the period from 1736 to around 1760. In the latter period, the Frenchman Pierre Perreault worked here as master type founder and taught the craft to several apprentices.

As a non-native newcomer, Christophe Plantin had experienced the need of tools for learning the Dutch language. He therefore published several dictionaries himself, as well as multilingual dialogues. For *Dialogues francois / Françoische t'samensprekinghen*, Plantin personally wrote two dialogues about printing. In simple language, he explained the complete printing process, from making the ink and paper, through typecasting, composing and proofreading, to the operation of the press. The two dialogues form the very first manual on the art of book printing, and they contain a wealth of information about printing techniques in the sixteenth century.

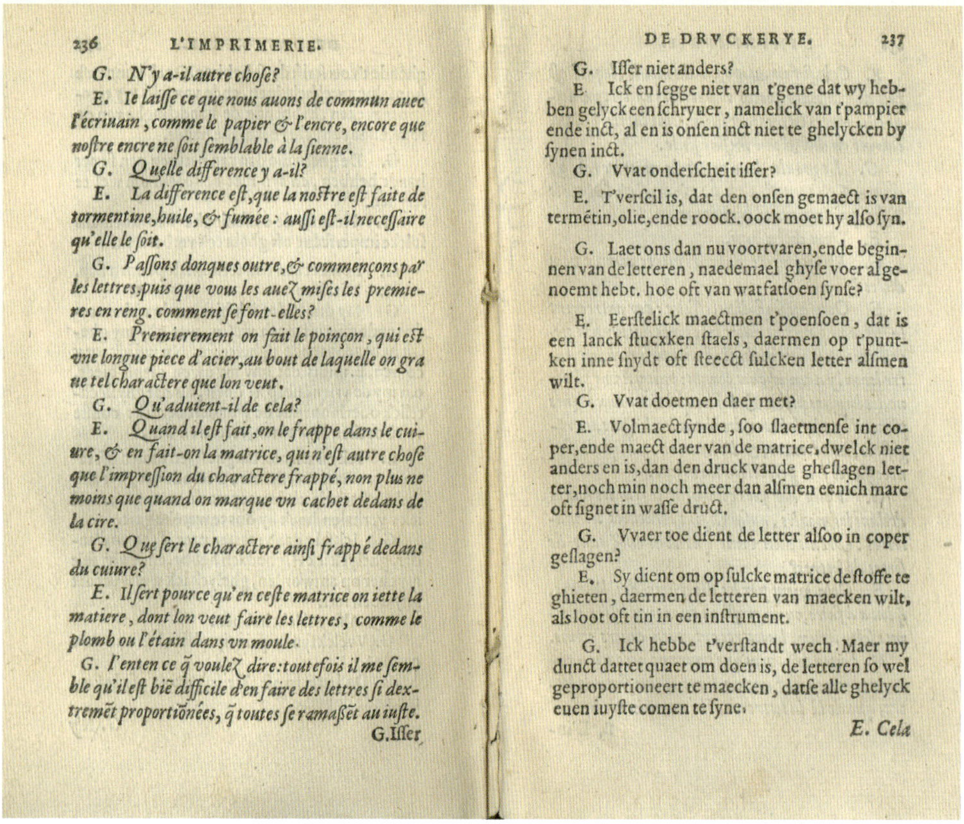

236 L'IMPRIMERIE.

G. N'y a-il autre choſe?

E. Ie laiſſe ce que nous auons de commun auec l'écriuain, comme le papier & l'encre, encore que noſtre encre ne ſoit ſemblable à la ſienne.

G. Quelle difference y a-il?

E. La difference eſt, que la noſtre eſt faite de tormentine, huile, & fumée: auſſi eſt-il neceſſaire qu'elle le ſoit.

G. Paſſons donques outre, & commençons par les lettres, puis que vous les auez miſes les premieres en reng. comment ſe font-elles?

E. Premierement on fait le poinçon, qui eſt vne longue piece d'acier, au bout de laquelle on graue tel charactere que lon veut.

G. Qu'aduient-il de cela?

E. Quand il eſt fait, on le frappe dans le cuiure, & en fait-on la matrice, qui n'eſt autre choſe que l'impreſſion du charactere frappé, non plus ne moins que quand on marque vn cachet dedans de la cire.

G. Que ſert le charactere ainſi frappé dedans du cuiure?

E. Il ſert pource qu'en ceſte matrice on iette la matiere, dont lon veut faire les lettres, comme le plomb ou l'étain dans vn moule.

G. I'enten ce q̃ voulez dire: toutefois il me ſemble qu'il eſt biẽ difficile d'en faire des lettres ſi dextremẽt proportiõnées, q̃ toutes ſe ramaſſẽt au iuſte.

G. Iſſer

DE DRVCKERYE. 237

G. Iſſer niet anders?

E. Ick en ſegge niet van t'gene dat wy hebben gelyck een ſchryuer, namelick van t'pampier ende inct, al en is onſen inct niet te ghelycken by ſynen inct.

G. Vvat onderſcheit iſſer?

E. T'verſcil is, dat den onſen gemaect is van termétin, olie, ende roock. oock moet hy alſo ſyn.

G. Laet ons dan nu voortvaren, ende beginnen van de letteren, naedemael ghyſe voer al genoemt hebt. hoe oft van watfatſoen ſynſe?

E. Eerſtelick maectmen t'poenſoen, dat is een lanck ſtucxken ſtaels, daermen op t'puntken inne ſnydt oft ſteect ſulcken letter alſmen wilt.

G. Vvat doetmen daer met?

E. Volmaect ſynde, ſoo ſlaetmenſe int coper, ende maect daer van de matrice, dwelck niet anders en is, dan den druck vande gheſlagen letter, noch min noch meer dan alſmen eenich marc oft ſignet in waſſe druct.

G. Vvaer toe dient de letter alſoo in coper geſlagen?

E. Sy dient om op ſulcke matrice de ſtoffe te ghieten, daermen de letteren van maecken wilt, als loot oft tin in een inſtrument.

G. Ick hebbe t'verſtandt wech. Maer my dunct dattet quaet om doen is, de letteren ſo wel geproportioneert te maecken, datſe alle ghelyck euen iuyſte comen te ſyne.

E. Cela

Librorum Prohibitorum Index, 1569. This list of prohibited books was compiled in great haste by Arias Montanus, on the order of the Duke of Alva. It is therefore very different to the later editions of the official index.

LIBRORVM PROHIBITORVM INDEX, EX MANDATO
REGIAE CATHOLICAE MAIESTA^tis^ ET ILLVSTRISS. DVCIS ALBANI,
CONSILIIQVE REGII DECRETO EDITVS.

ANTVERPIAE, EXCVDEBAT CHRISTOPHORV ... M. D. LXIX.

Printing room: the eighteenth high-pressure press.

The *woodcutters* and *engravers* also worked elsewhere. *Graphic designers* usually made sketches of the illustrations required. At the request of his old friend Balthasar Moretus, the renowned painter Peter Paul Rubens made several designs for book illustrations. The woodcutters cut the design into a block of wood and the engravers etched or engraved the design into a copper plate. Plantin and his followers paid the graphic artists for piece-work. In Plantin's day, printing the engravings and etchings was contracted out to the artist's studio, as a special high-pressure press is needed to print copper plates. It was only in the eighteenth century that the Plantin printing house started to use such a press. Woodblocks, however, were always fitted in between the type in the matrix and printed together with the text.

There were no *bookbinders* working at the Plantin printing house. Customers usually bought their books unbound as a sheaf of separate quires, but if they did want a binding Plantin had the copy bound elsewhere.
As an exception, Plantin made luxury bindings himself for distinguished people or wealthy book-lovers, as he had worked as a bookbinder before taking up the career of printer.

The *Officina Plantiniana* was a family firm. Plantin married off some of his daughters to loyal employees. His eldest daughter Margareta married Franciscus Raphelengius, who worked as a proofreader in the printing house and was an expert in Hebrew and Arabic. Martina married her father's right-hand man Jan Moretus, who was in charge of correspondence and sales, as well as doing the accounts. Both sons-in-law lived with their

PP. 114–115: Robert Péril, *The triumphal procession of Emperor Charles V and Pope Clement VII, in Bologna, on 24 February 1530*. It is the only known copy of this monumental woodcut on parchment, made by printmaker Robert Péril. He worked as an eyewitness for the sister of Emperor Charles, Margaret of Austria.

families in Plantin's house, and other employees also had the opportunity to live there, on deduction of a sum for bed and board from their wages. It was mainly bachelors who chose this option. The well-known proof-reader Cornelis Kiliaan, for example, lived in Plantin's house for nearly fifty years. It was also usual for apprentices to lodge with Plantin for the duration of their apprenticeship. So it was sometimes rather a tight squeeze with so many people living together.

The employees of Plantin's printing house worked long days of fourteen hours. The working day started at 6 o'clock in the morning, and for the 'premiers' even at 5 o'clock. There was an hour's lunch break between 12 and 1 o'clock, besides which the employees were entitled to two half-hour breaks between 8 and 9 o'clock and between 4 and 5 o'clock in the afternoon.
The working day ended at 8 o'clock in the evening. After subtracting the break hours, the employees effectively worked for twelve and a half hours a day. There were six working days a week, and the employees were free only on Sundays and holidays.

Above the two oldest printing presses in the world hangs a terracotta statue of the Virgin Mary, representing Our Lady of Loreto. In the Middle Ages, the home of the Virgin Mary had been miraculously transported from the Holy Land to the small Italian town of Loreto, whereupon a basilica was promptly built around it. Loreto rapidly grew into a place of pilgrimage that attracted visitors from all over the world.
On his trip to Italy in 1664, Balthasar III Moretus visited the basilica, and the statue of Mary in the printing house undoubtedly reminded him of his visit. A candle was lit next to the statue during working hours. The Kapel master of the 'Kleine Bus' decorated the statue, for which he received voluntary contributions from the journeymen.

EGO ILLE SVM : CAROLVS QVINTVS HOC : NOMINE : CAESAR NATVS AD IMPERIVM
OPPRESSOS RELEVARE MANV FRENARE SVPERBOS : CONSILIIS

ERE LEGES : LAPSA : TRIBVNATIVM : IVS PRISCOSQVE QVIRITES : PATRICIOS : REVOQVARE : VIROS
OMNIA ETERVM SERVATO : TRAMITE TRAMITE MORVM : IN

VT SCEPTRA TENEREM EST ANIMVS FOSSAS
VE MEIS IVRISQVE VETVSTI LEGIBVS
LIBERTAS

SANCTVMQVE SENATVM ET REDDERE PRIMEVO
ANTIQVAM CORRECTA DEDUCERE PACEM

Since most employees were paid for piece-work, they could not earn anything on their free days. On Saturdays, they were paid their wages for the work they had completed that week.

Since the Middle Ages, craftsmen in towns and cities had been organising themselves by profession in guilds. After the invention of printing, book printers in Antwerp joined the existing Guild of Saint Luke for artists. Although they did not like it at the beginning, later on they dominated the guild. Christophe Plantin was also a member of the Guild of Saint Luke, and at the beginning of the seventeenth century, his grandson Jan II Moretus even led the guild for a few years as dean. Membership of the Guild of Saint Luke was reserved for the masters. Journeymen were excluded and they had their own association within the

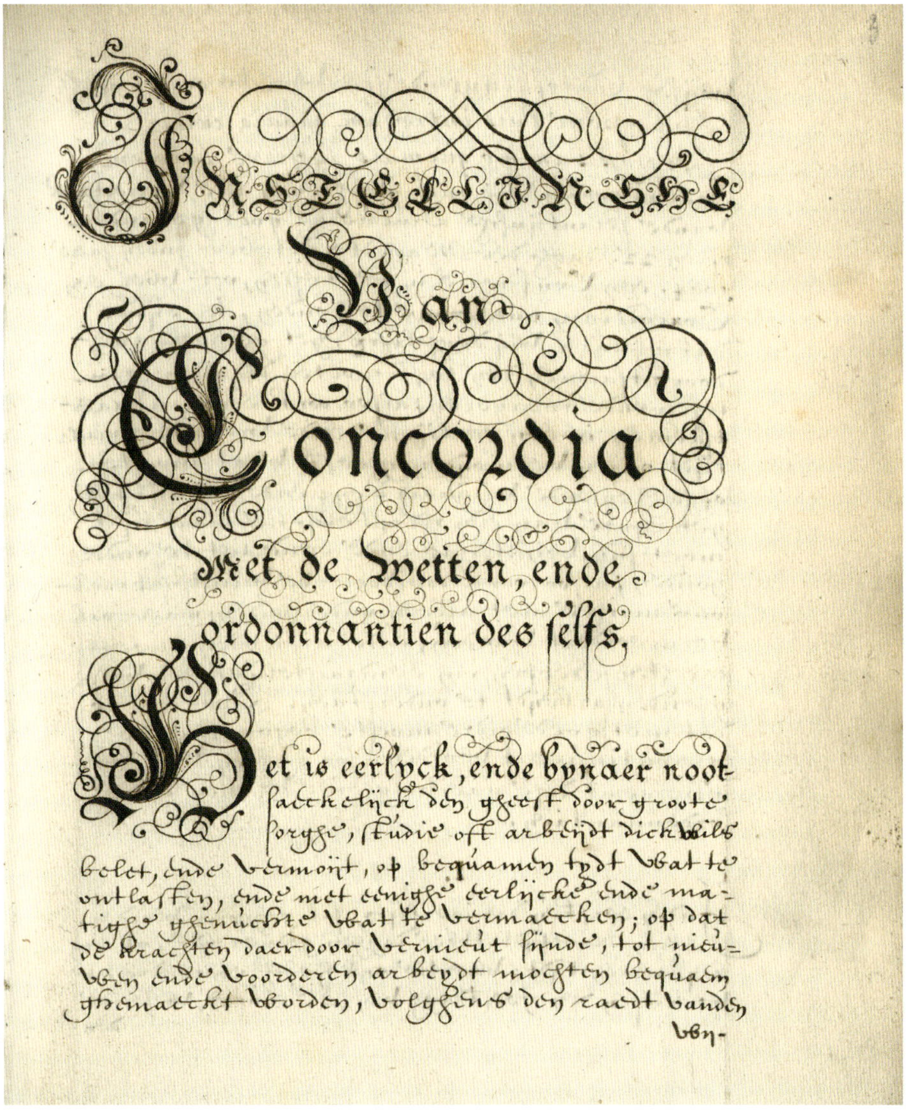
Instellinghe
Van
Concordia
Met de Wetten, ende
ordonnantien des selfs,
Het is eerlyck, ende bynaer noot-
saeckelijck den ghenen door groote
sorghe, studie oft arbeydt dickwils
belet, ende vermoeyt, op bequamen tydt wat te
ontlasten, ende met eenighe eerlijcke ende ma-
tighe ghenuchte wat te vermaecken; op dat
de krachten daer door vernieut synde, tot nieu-
wen ende voorderen arbeydt mochten bequaem
ghemaeckt worden, volghens den raedt vanden
wyn-

Incipit of the articles of association of the *Concordia* fraternity, 1666.

Plantin printing house, which was generally referred to by the term 'Kapel' (chapel). All over Europe, printing journeymen united within their firm in this type of organisation, the earliest traces of which are found in the Plantin archive. The name probably came from an association of printing journeymen in Paris, who held their meetings in the chapel of Saint-Jean-de-Latran in the first half of the sixteenth century.

The Kapel at the *Officina Plantiniana* was approved by Christophe Plantin, as the master could largely entrust it to keep law and order on the shop floor. It also gave him a point of contact for his many employees. All the printers and compositors were obliged to become members of the Kapel through an initiation ceremony. The proofreaders and shop assistants, however, could not become members. In the heart of the Kapel, Plantin established a health service, which gave financial support to sick members and to the relatives of deceased members. It was funded by fines and by contributions from the master and his employees. The master paid a

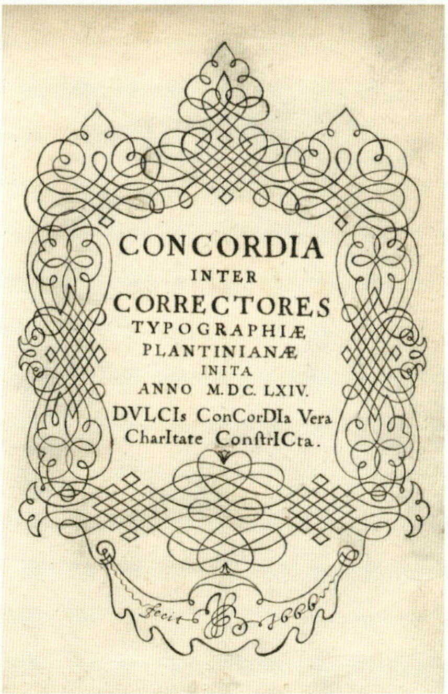

Following the example of the printers and compositors, the proofreaders established their own fraternity in 1664. The association was given the euphonic name 'Concordia inter correctores typographiae Plantinianae' (concord between the proofreaders of the Plantin printing house). According to the articles, which were written in beautiful calligraphy, the fraternity held a celebration every year on 18 October. First, the members attended Mass in honour of their patron saint, St Luke. Then they enjoyed a copious meal at the home of one of the members, who took in turn to hold the annual celebration at their home. It was paid for by a combination of one-off and weekly contributions from the members.

fixed three-monthly amount for each press. The master also dug deep in his pockets in the case of exceptional family circumstances. Midway through the seventeenth century, a reorganisation split the health service in two. The function of health service was taken on by the 'Grote Bus' and the payments for exceptional circumstances were made by the 'Kleine Bus'. After a while, the 'Grote Bus' became so wealthy that it invested its capital in interest on houses and also gave loans to its members.

The board of the Kapel – called the 'Wet' – was reappointed annually. The board was democratically elected by and from the members of the Kapel. The head of the Kapel, who chaired the Wet, was called the prince or captain. Two solicitors formed the armed force of the Wet, and the health

Recently, descendants of the Moretuses presented the museum with a mysterious family heirloom. Put irreverently, it looks like a painted cricket bat. The item was probably used in the initiation rite of the new journeymen. After a trial period of one year and six weeks, the new printers and compositors were 'freed' in an obligatory baptism ceremony. The prince of the Kapel led the initiation with the beautifully decorated ceremonial paddle. Beer flowed in abundance at the expense of the newcomers. While singing the baptismal song, the godfathers would spank the new journeymen with the paddle and pour water over them, singing 'Een nieuw Liedt soo heffen wy aen, Wy willen hier een de Brits gaen slaen ... Hier gieten die Peters water ende gheven den Naem' (And so we break into a new song. We'll spank him with the paddle. The godfathers will pour water and give him a name).

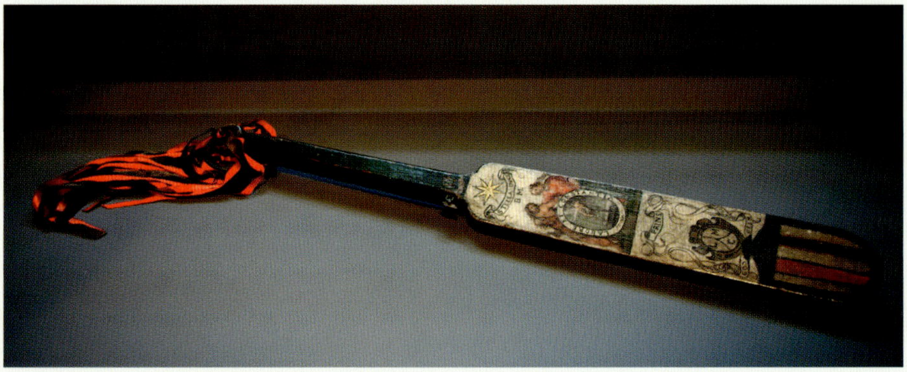

Baptismal song that was sung at the initiation ceremony of the journeymen, seventeenth century.

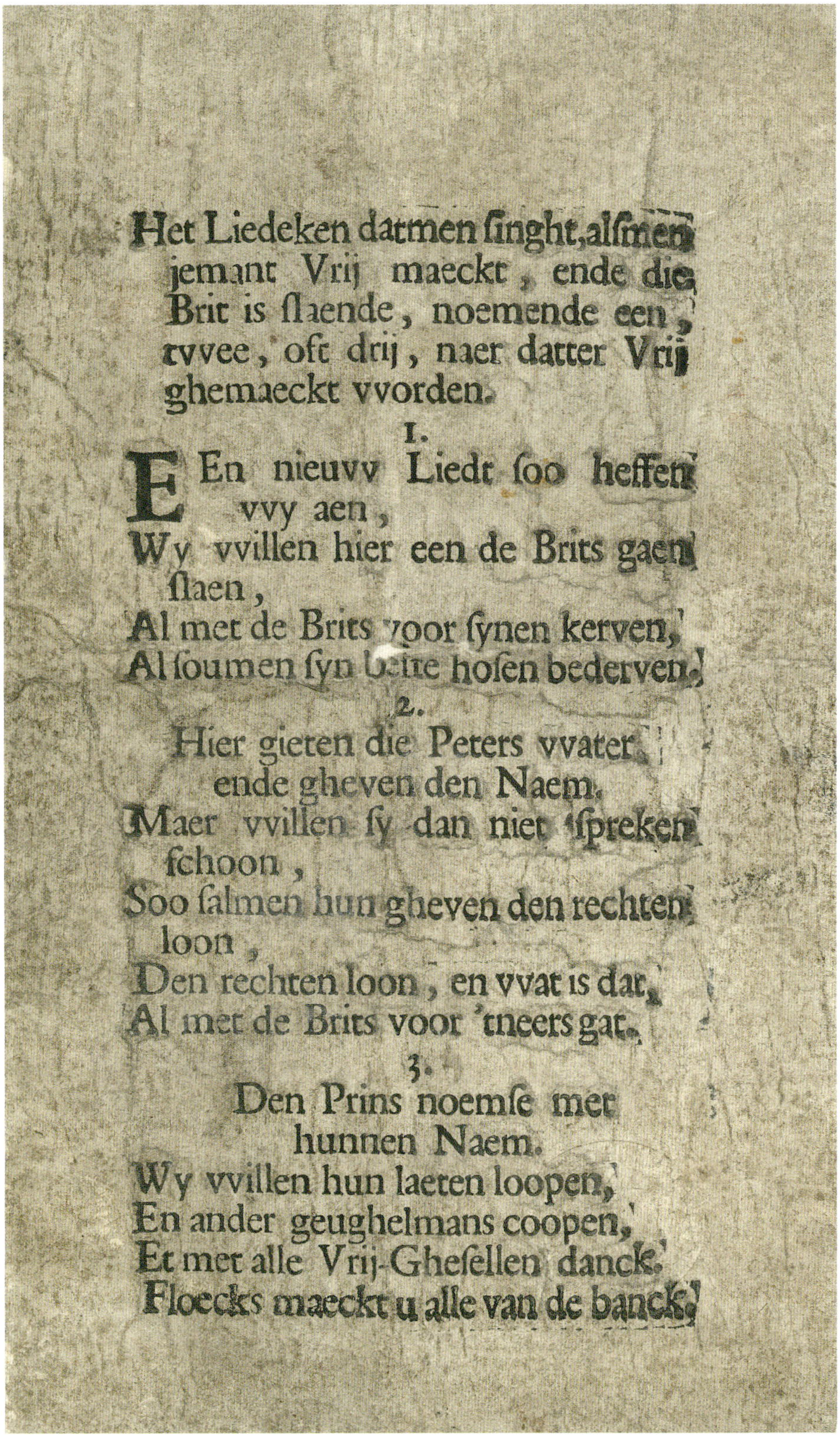

Het Liedeken datmen ſinght, alſmen jemant Vrij maeckt, ende die Brit is ſlaende, noemende een, tvvee, oft drij, naer datter Vrij ghemaeckt vvorden.

1.

En nieuvv Liedt ſoo heffen vvy aen,
Wy vvillen hier een de Brits gaen ſlaen,
Al met de Brits voor ſynen kerven,
Al ſoumen ſyn beſte hoſen bederven.

2.

Hier gieten die Peters vvater ende gheven den Naem.
Maer vvillen ſy dan niet ſpreken ſchoon,
Soo ſalmen hun gheven den rechten loon,
Den rechten loon, en vvat is dat,
Al met de Brits voor 'tneers gat.

3.

Den Prins noemſe met hunnen Naem.
Wy vvillen hun laeten loopen,
En ander geughelmans coopen,
Et met alle Vrij-Gheſellen danck,
Floecks maeckt u alle van de banck.

Journael

van de Rekeninghe der Busse
van de Ghesellen der Plantijnsche
Druckerije tot solaes ende assi-
stentie van de siecke, beghinnen-
de den eersten Meert 1653.

Geteeckent A

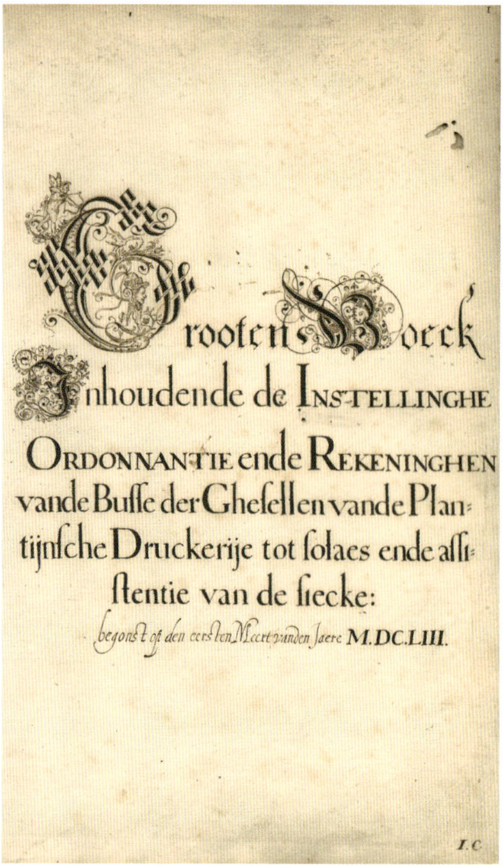

Grooten Boeck
Inhoudende de Instellinghe
Ordonnantie ende Rekeninghen
vande Busse der Ghesellen vande Plan-
tijnsche Druckerije tot solaes ende assi-
stentie van de siecke:
begonst op den eersten Meert vanden Jaere M.DC.LIII.

I.C

Journal of the health service of the Plantin printing house, 1653.

Ledger and articles of association of the health service of the Plantin printing house, 1653.

service accounts were done by the masters of the Kleine Bus and the Grote Bus. Every year, the secretary noted down the new composition of the Wet and kept the complaints book up to date. Members could only be exempted from a board mandate by exception; for example in the case of an illiterate printer being elected secretary. The Wet held a meeting every three months, chaired by the prince. The Wet was authorised to issue new working regulations and to impose disciplinary measures. In Plantin's day, the working regulations were issued by the master himself.

These working regulations or orders of the Plantin printing house are interesting historical documents. In the first regulations from around 1555, Plantin forbade practical jokes like putting a sponge under someone's backside. Anyone breaking this rule had to pay for a pitcher of ale. In later orders, the beer was replaced by a fine to be paid to the Kapel. Only the apprentices could get a hiding if, for example, they neglected to sweep out the printing house on Sundays. In the days of the Moretuses, any breach of the regulations was written down in the complaints book. The secretary also noted down the reciprocal complaints of the journeymen. The Wet judged the complaints and handed out any fines to the offenders. The complaints books are an interesting source of information about daily life on the shop floor. In the mid-eighteenth century, the Kapel faded out, although the health service remained in operation until at least 1808.

The new composition of the board of the 'Kapel' of the *Officina Plantiniana*, 1721.

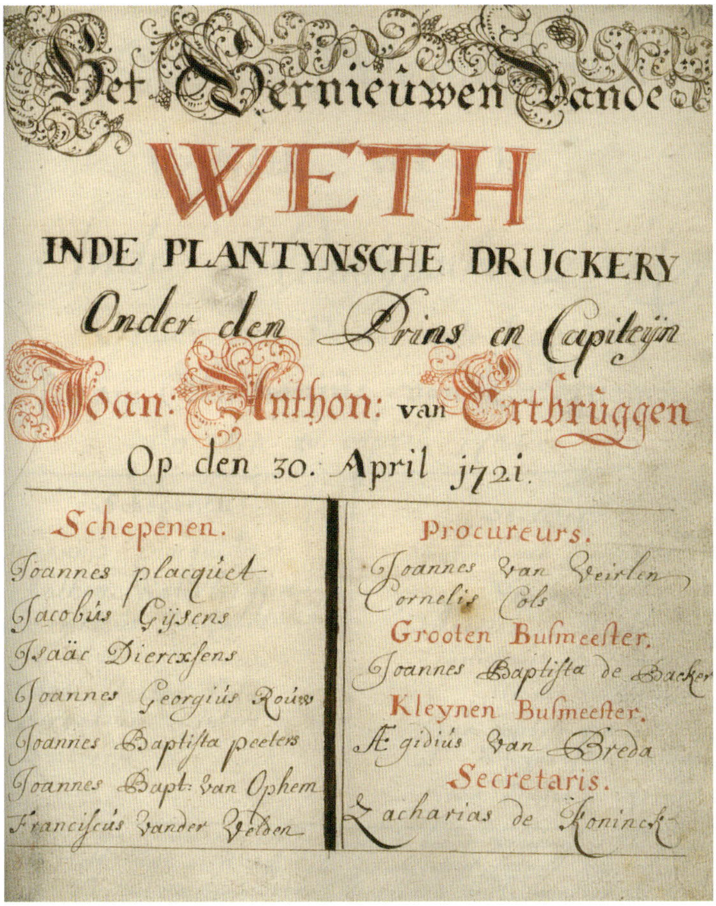

Het Vernieuwen Vande

WETH

INDE PLANTYNSCHE DRUCKERY

Onder den Prins en Capiteyn

Joan: Anthon: van Erthrüggen

Op den 30. April 1721.

Schepenen.	Procureurs.
Joannes placquet	Joannes van Veirlen
Jacobus Gysens	Cornelis Cols
Isaäc Diercxsens	Grooten Busmeester.
Joannes Georgius Rouw	Joannes Baptista de Backer
Joannes Baptista peeters	Kleynen Busmeester.
Joannes Bapt: van Ophem	Ægidius van Breda
Franciscus vander Velden	Secretaris.
	Zacharias de Koninck

In the days of the Moretuses, any breach of the regulations was written down in the complaints book. The secretary also noted down the reciprocal complaints of the journeymen. Every three months, the board of the Kapel judged the complaints and handed out any fines to the offenders. The complaints books provide a lot of information about daily life on the shop floor. For instance, we were able to reconstruct the following childish discussion:

Francis: You're a filthy lecher!
Jacobus: No, you're a filthy lecher!
Francis: I never said filthy lecher!
Jacobus: You told the captain I made a fool of him 1000 times today, didn't you?
Francis: That's not true, and the captain's witness to it!

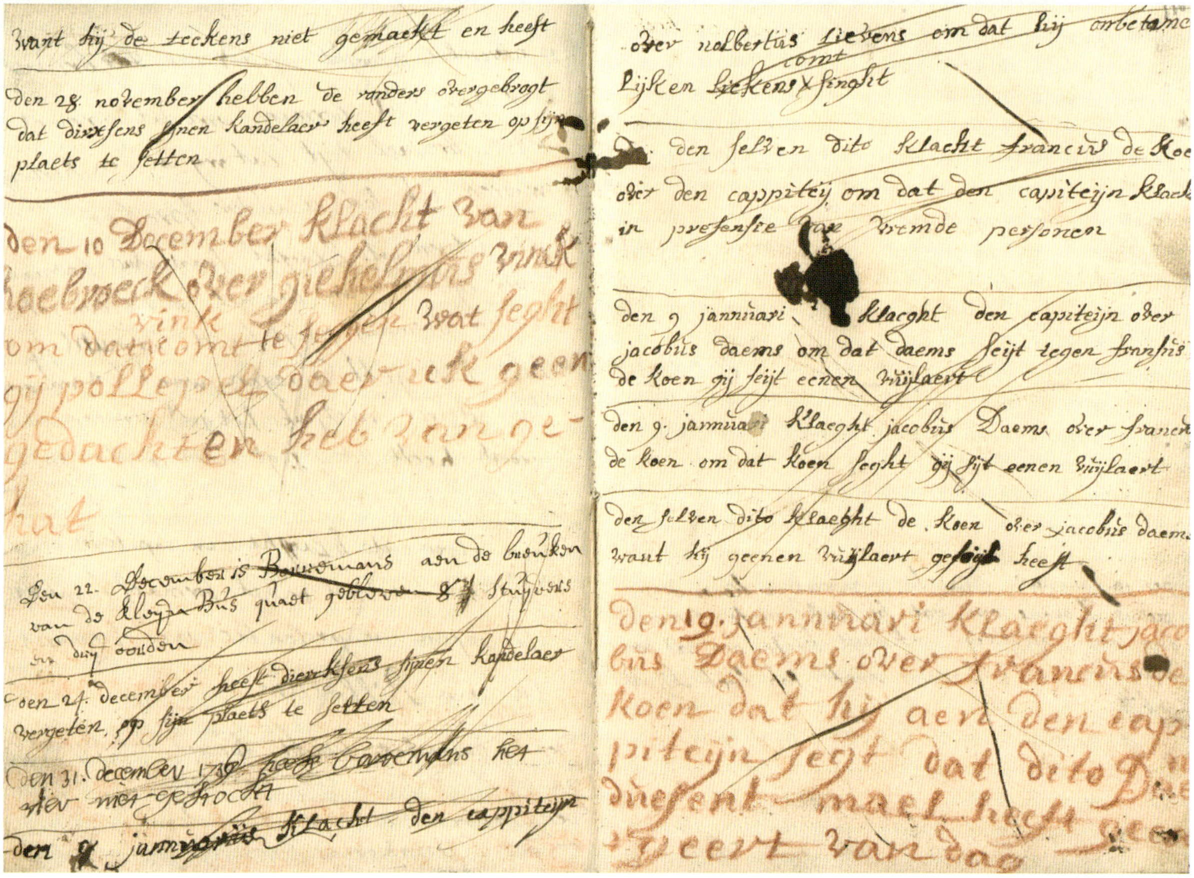
want hij de teekens niet gemaekt en heeft

den 28 november hebben de randers overgebrogt dat dirksens sijnen kandelaer heeft vergeten op sijn plaets te setten

den 10 December klacht van hoebroeck over giehelmus vink om dat vink comt te seggen wat seght gij pollepel daer ick geen gedachten heb van ge-hat

den 22 December is Bouwmans aen de boucken van de kloghBus quaet gebleven 8 stuyvers

den 24 december heeft dierksens sijnen kandelaer vergeten op sijn plaets te setten

den 31 december 17.. heeft bouwmans het ... mee gebrocht

den 9 jannuari klacht den cappiteijn

over albertus lievens om dat hij onbetamelijken comt teekens singht

den selven dito klacht francus de koen over den cappiteij om dat den capiteijn klacht in presensie van vremde personen

den 9 jannuari klaght den capiteijn over jacobus daems om dat daems seijt tegen fransis de koen gij seijt eenen vuijlaert

den 9 jannuari klaeght jacobus Daems over francis de koen om dat koen seght gij sijt eenen vuijlaert

den selven dito klaeght de koen over jacobus daems want hij geenen vuijlaert gesijt heeft

den 9 jannuari klaeght jacobus Daems over francus de koen dat hij aen den cappiteijn seght dat dito Daems duijsent mael heeft geeckgeert vandaeg

The first working regulations of the Plantin printing house, c. 1555–1556.

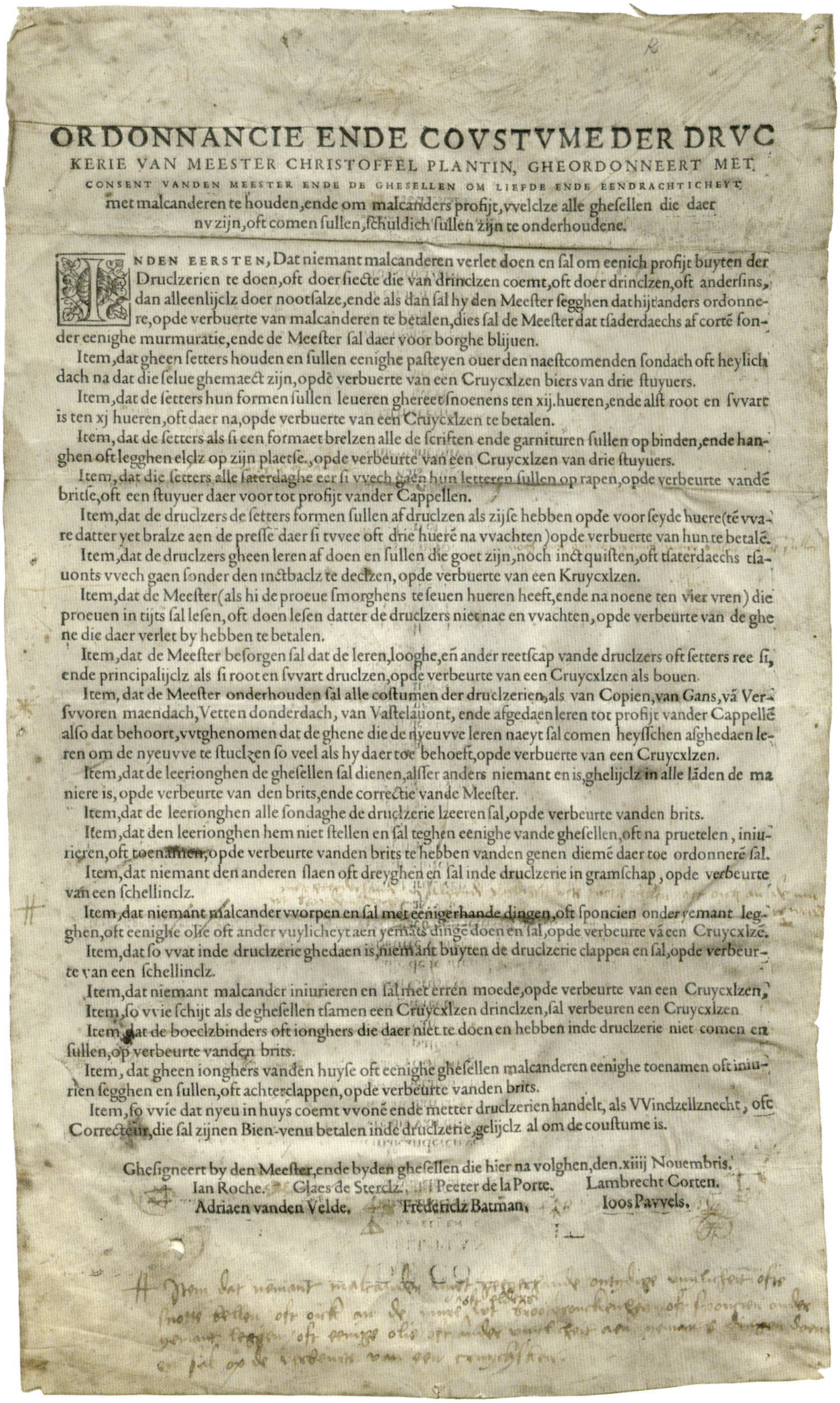

ORDONNANCIE ENDE COVSTVME DER DRVC KERIE VAN MEESTER CHRISTOFFEL PLANTIN, GHEORDONNEERT MET CONSENT VANDEN MEESTER ENDE DE GHESELLEN OM LIEFDE ENDE EENDRACHTICHEYT met malcanderen te houden, ende om malcanders profijt, vvelcke alle ghesellen die daer nv zijn, oft comen ſullen, ſchuldich ſullen zijn te onderhoudene.

INDEN EERSTEN, Dat niemant malcanderen verlet doen en ſal om eenich profijt buyten der Druckerien te doen, oft doer ſiecte die van drincken coemt, oft doer drincken, oft anderſins, dan alleenlijck doer nootſake, ende als dan ſal hy den Meeſter ſegghen dat hijt anders ordonnere, opde verbuerte van malcanderen te betalen, dies ſal de Meeſter dat tſaderdaechs af cortẽ ſonder eenighe murmuratie, ende de Meeſter ſal daer voor borghe blijuen.

Item, dat gheen ſetters houden en ſullen eenighe paſteyen ouer den naeſtcomenden ſondach oft heylich dach na dat die ſelue ghemaect zijn, opdẽ verbuerte van een Cruycxken biers van drie ſtuyuers.

Item, dat de ſetters hun formen ſullen leueren ghereet ſnoenens ten xij. hueren, ende alſt root en ſvvart is ten xj hueren, oft daer na, opde verbuerte van een Cruycxken te betalen.

Item, dat de ſetters als ſi een formaet breken alle de ſcriften ende garnituren ſullen op binden, ende hanghen oft legghen elck op zijn plaetſe., opde verbeurte van een Cruycxken van drie ſtuyuers.

Item, dat die ſetters alle ſaterdaghe eer ſi vvech gaen hun letteren ſullen op rapen, opde verbeurte vandẽ britſe, oft een ſtuyuer daer voor tot profijt vander Cappellen.

Item, dat de druckers de ſetters formen ſullen af drucken als zijſe hebben opde voor ſeyde huere (tẽ vvare datter yet brake aen de preſſe daer ſi tvvee oft drie huerẽ na vvachten) opde verbuerte van hun te betalẽ.

Item, dat de druckers gheen leren af doen en ſullen die goet zijn, noch inct quiſten, oft tſaterdaechs tſauonts vvech gaen ſonder den inctback te decken, opde verbuerte van een Kruycxken.

Item, dat de Meeſter (als hi de proeue ſmorghens te ſeuen hueren heeft, ende na noene ten vier vren) die proeuen in tijts ſal leſen, oft doen leſen datter de druckers niet nae en vvachten, opde verbeurte van de ghene die daer verlet by hebben te betalen.

Item, dat de Meeſter beſorgen ſal dat de leren, looghe, eñ ander reetſcap vande druckers oft ſetters ree ſi, ende principalijck als ſi root en ſvvart drucken, opde verbeurte van een Cruycxken als bouen.

Item, dat de Meeſter onderhouden ſal alle coſtumen der druckerien, als van Copien, van Gans, vã Verſvvoren maendach, Vetten donderdach, van Vaſtelauont, ende afgedaen leren tot profijt vander Cappellẽ alſo dat behoort, vvtghenomen dat de ghene die de nyeuvve leren naeyt ſal comen heyſſchen afghedaen leren om de nyeuvve te ſtucken ſo veel als hy daer toe behoeft, opde verbuerte van een Cruycxken.

Item, dat de leerionghen de gheſellen ſal dienen, alſſer anders niemant en is, ghelijck in alle lãden de maniere is, opde verbeurte van den brits, ende correctie vande Meeſter.

Item, dat de leerionghen alle ſondaghe de druckerie keeren ſal, opde verbeurte vanden brits.

Item, dat den leerionghen hem niet ſtellen en ſal teghen eenighe vande gheſellen, oft na pruetelen, iniurieren, oft toenamen, opde verbeurte vanden brits te hebben vanden genen diemẽ daer toe ordonnerẽ ſal.

Item, dat niemant den anderen ſlaen oft dreyghen en ſal inde druckerie in gramſchap, opde verbeurte van een ſchellinck.

Item, dat niemant malcander vvorpen en ſal met eenigerhande dingen, oft ſponcien onder yemant legghen, oft eenighe olie oft ander vuylicheyt aen yemãts dingẽ doen en ſal, opde verbeurte vã een Cruycxkẽ.

Item, dat ſo vvat inde druckerie ghedaen is, niemant buyten de druckerie clappen en ſal, opde verbeurte van een ſchellinck.

Item, dat niemant malcander iniurieren en ſal met erren moede, opde verbeurte van een Cruycxken.

Item, ſo vvie ſchijt als de gheſellen tſamen een Cruycxken drincken, ſal verbeuren een Cruycxken

Item, dat de boeckbinders oft ionghers die daer niet te doen en hebben inde druckerie niet comen en ſullen, op verbeurte vanden brits.

Item, dat gheen ionghers vanden huyſe oft eenighe gheſellen malcanderen eenighe toenamen oft iniurien ſegghen en ſullen, oft achterclappen, opde verbeurte vanden brits.

Item, ſo vvie dat nyeu in huys coemt vvonẽ ende metter druckerien handelt, als VVinckelknecht, oft Correcteur, die ſal zijnen Bien-venu betalen inde druckerie, gelijck al om de couſtume is.

Gheſigneert by den Meeſter, ende byden gheſellen die hier na volghen, den. xiiij Nouembris.

Ian Roche. Claes de Sterck. Peeter de la Porte. Lambrecht Corten.

Adriaen vanden Velde. Frederick Batman. Ioos Pavvels.

The Golden Compass

Iris Kockelbergh & Kris Geysen

Plantin's business grew rapidly and he kept moving to bigger premises. It was only in 1576 that he moved into the house on Vrijdagmarkt. He lived there until his death in 1589, after which the most skilled sons always inherited the house along with the printing business. Nine generations of printers kept the business running and made their mark on the house, which represents a mode of living that spans exactly three hundred years. In 1876, the family sold the premises, which opened as a museum one year later.

Before setting up at Vrijdagmarkt, Plantin lived at various addresses

1548–1549 - Lombardenvest: Plantin is a bookbinder
1552 - Twaalfmaandenstraat: Plantin installs his first printing press and prints *La institutione di una fanciulla nata nobilmente*
1557 - Kammenstraat: he renames *De Gulden Eenhoorn* (The Golden Unicorn) as *De Gulden Passer* (The Golden Compass), where he prints *La magnifique et somptueuse Pompe Funèbre*
1560 - Kammenstraat: between Bergstraat and Gierstraat, Plantin takes possession of the *Grote Valck* (The Large Falcon) and the *Kleine Valck* (The Small Falcon), and the *Bettel* (The Cisel). Soon he owns a total of seven houses, where he prints his masterpiece, the *Biblia Regia*.
1576 - Vrijdagmarkt/Hoogstraat: Plantin rents a large building with an entrance on Hoogstraat and exit onto Vrijdagmarkt. Three years later, he buys the part of the house on Vrijdagmarkt, where he prints Guicciardini's *Description de touts les Pais-Bas.*

'Enen ... groote huysinghe met poorte, gaelderye, plaetse, toren, salette, ceuckene, ... een groote plaetse, borneputte, regenbacke en bleykhove ende enen cruythove, met een groote neercamere, diverssche oppercameren, comptoiren, stallinge, washuyse, comende ... achter uuyte met eender grooter poorter opte Vrydaeghs Merct met een poortcamere daer boven ende een nedercamere daer neffens met veele andere diverssche oppercameren, solders ende kelders, gronde ..., gestaen ende gelegen inde Hoochstraete.'

'A... large house with gate, gallery, yard, tower, parlour, kitchen with another large yard, a well, water cistern, bleaching yard, vegetable garden, with one large downstairs room, various upstairs rooms, offices, stables, wash house... the same building also gives out onto the Vrijdagmarkt through a large gate with one room above and another next to it, with many other upstairs rooms, attics and cellars, grounds... situated in Hoogstraat.'

In 1576 Plantin signed the lease for a new *Gulden Passer* – or Golden Compass – on Hoogstraat. His printing shop in the cramped building on Kammenstraat was bursting at the seams. Generations of the Plantin-Moretus family lived in the *Gulden Passer* for 300 years until they sold it to the City of Antwerp in 1876.

Virgilius Bononiensis, *City map of Antwerp in aerial view*, 1555, Museum Plantin-Moretus, showing the places where Plantin lived and worked.

Newcomer Plantin finds his feet

PERIOD 1548–1576

1548 Plantin moved from Paris to Antwerp with his wife and child. Here he set himself up as a bookbinder on Lombardenvest in the printers' and booksellers' quarter. One of the streets there is still called Drukkerijstraat – or Printers' Street – today.

1552 Plantin moved to Twaalfmaandenstraat near the Stock Exchange. It was there that in 1555 he printed his first work, *La institutione di una fanciulla nata nobilmente*, about a noble girl's education.

1557 Five years later he was to be found at the *Gouden Eenhoorn* (Golden Unicorn) in Kammenstraat where he printed a short text for the publication about Emperor Charles V's funeral procession. *La magnifique et somptueuse Pompe funèbre... du tresgrand et tresvictorieus Charles Cinquième...* appeared in 1559. Hieronymus Cock printed the thirty-three engravings, which together form a twelve-metre-long frieze. Plantin's name as a printer was established.

1561 Plantin renamed his house the *Gulden Passer*. A Calvinist pamphlet turned up in his printing house. Plantin went into hiding in Paris. All his possessions were seized and auctioned off on the Vrijdagmarkt. Activity at the company came to a standstill.

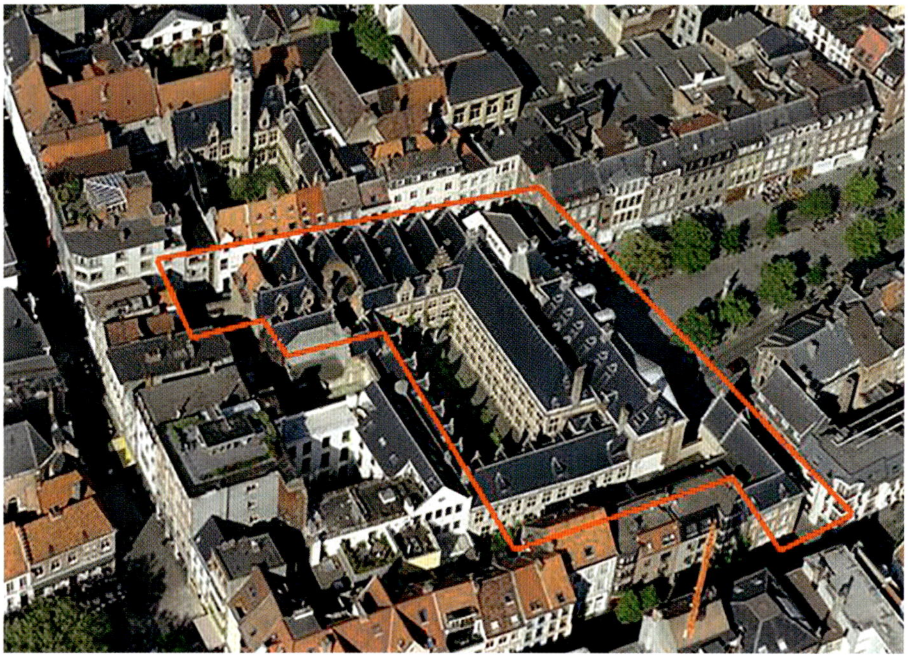

Aerial photo of the complete site of the Museum Plantin-Moretus.

1563 With the help of several partners Plantin was back in business.

1565 The printing house went from strength to strength and Plantin moved to the *Grote Valk* (The Large Falcon), the *Kleine Valk* (The Small Falcon) and the *Beitel* (Chisel) round the corner from Kammenstraat and Gierstraat. The name of his company moved with him. From then on the *Grote Valk* was called the *Gulden Passer*. It was in this group of houses that Plantin produced his greatest masterpiece: the famous *Biblia polyglotta* or *Biblia Regia* in five languages, Latin, Greek, Hebrew, Aramaic and Old Syriac. The *Officina Plantiniana* blossomed and flourished. By 1576 the company owned seven buildings in Kammenstraat. The Carmelite monastery was used for storing a part of his stock of books.

1575 Plantin became the largest printing establishment in Europe, boasting sixteen presses and almost eighty employees.

1576 Plantin signed a lease for the complex on Hoogstraat, with the exit on the Vrijdagmarkt. The bookshop remained in Kammenstraat, a 'commercial' shopping street with a good footfall.

PP. 132–133: Printing room seen from the garden.

A permanent home for the Gulden Passer

PERIOD 1576–1589

1576 A couple of months after the move, the Spanish Fury raged through the city. Plantin's company escaped the plundering, but the unstable political situation caused a severe recession in Antwerp. The printing house saw a substantial downturn in business.

1579 The owner split the large rented house on Hoogstraat in two. Plantin bought the smaller part, overlooking the Vrijdagmarkt. He was now the owner of the large garden, but was short of living space. The house comprised:

- an office
- one large living area (what is today the Lipsius Room)
- a wash house on the ground floor
- several small rooms upstairs
- a coach house exiting onto Heilige Geeststraat
- a gatehouse overlooking the Vrijdagmarkt, with a drawing-room downstairs and a room upstairs.

There were still seven small houses to the right of the gatehouse. They didn't belong to

Floor plan of the house and the surrounding premises.

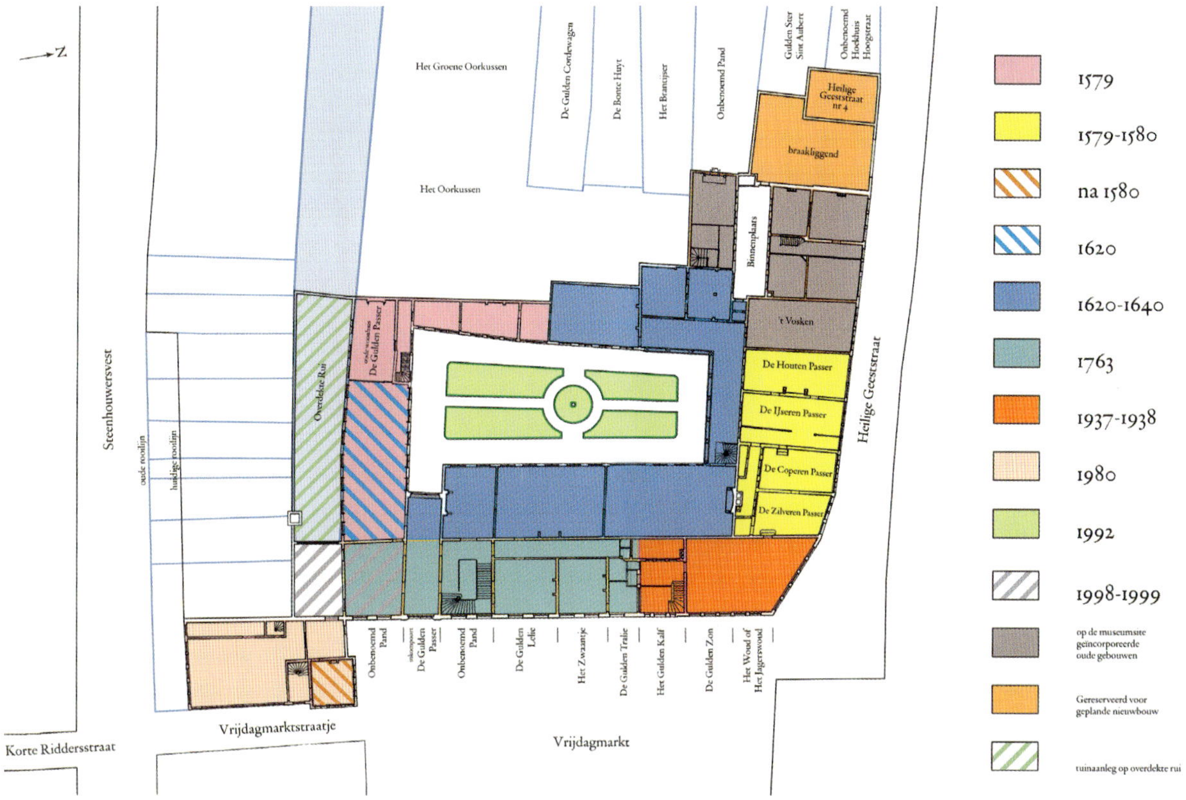

PLANTINUS
LABORE ET CONSTANTIA

Row of houses in Heilige Geeststraat, including the *Wooden*, *Iron*, *Copper* and *Silver Compass*, built by Christophe Plantin.

Plantin. Over time the family bought them one by one. Plantin and his family lived in a very small space above the business premises, which was not unusual in those days. His eldest daughter Marguerite, for example, lived with her husband, three children and a maid in a single room in Kammenstraat measuring less than 16 m^2.
In his new property there was little space for printing presses. Initially this did not present a problem. The economic malaise which followed the Spanish Fury meant that Plantin only needed five presses.
By 1580 he had seven presses in operation, a year later eight. Again Plantin found himself short of space. He had a large room built for his printing presses on the canal side.
1580 Plantin built four rental houses on the Heilige Geeststraat side. The *Zilveren Passer* (Silver Compass) replaced the old coach house, next to it came the *Koperen Passer* (Copper Compass), the *IJzeren Passer* (Iron Compass) and the *Houten Passer* (Wooden Compass).
The city wanted to cover over the open sewers of the canal on Geeststraat and allowed residents who contributed

The corner house once built by Plantin, which was destroyed in 1945, photo 1972.

Jan II Moretus died in 1618, leaving behind his three-year-old son, Balthasar II. As godfather, Balthasar I looked after the boy's upbringing. From the diaries of Balthasar II, it appears that the two were very close. His uncle allowed Balthasar II to lay the foundation stone of the big extensions to the house on Vrijdagmarkt in 1620 and 1637. In two big projects, Uncle Balthasar extended the house into a stately mansion. He built the galleries on the courtyard, added new drawing rooms and constructed an extra floor on top of the printing house. Whereas his friend Rubens had a Baroque city palace erected, Balthasar I opted for the more austere Renaissance style, which was better suited to what his grandfather had built.

financially to use the land that became available. Plantin seized the opportunity to build a small house on the former canal next to the gatehouse. This may have become the correctors' room. During the Second World War, in 1945, that house was almost completely destroyed. Plantin created two additional entrances to his premises, one via Hoogstraat and the *Bonte Huid* land, and one via the *IJzeren Passer* in Heilige Geeststraat.

1582 Plantin's ambitions extended beyond Antwerp. In Leiden he founded a second printing cum publishing house. His son-in-law Raphelengius built up that business. He specialized in oriental printing, such as Arabic. In Antwerp Plantin was racking up large profits with his many Catholic publications, which included bibles, prayer books and liturgical works. He also printed major works by some of the Low Countries' greatest scholars, such as Ortelius' atlases.

1589 On 1 July 1589 the famous publisher died. His estate comprised:

- the main house the *Gulden Passer*, including the gatehouse, the small house in the left-hand corner of the Vrijdagmarkt and the small house on the other side of the gatehouse
- four houses in Kammenstraat/Gierstraat
- four rental houses in Heilige Geeststraat
- a garden retreat in Berchem
- the printing house in Leiden.

His successor and son-in-law Jan I Moretus inherited the *Gulden Passer*, the garden in Berchem and the *Grote Valk* in Kammenstraat. His son-in-law Raphelengius inherited the publishing house in Leiden. The rest of the Antwerp estate went to the other sons-in-law or was sold.

Bricked-up door under the portrait bust of Balthasar IV Moretus, at the entrance to the enfilade of the three drawing rooms built by Balthasar I Moretus. When the big classical wing had been built, this entrance was closed off.

From father to son Jan I and Balthasar I Moretus

PERIOD 1589–1641

In 1608 son-in-law Jan I Moretus bought the *Houten Passer*. After his death, his son Jan II Moretus took over the bookshop. His second son, Balthasar I, became the new director of the printing business and moved into the main house. The artistically-inclined Balthasar I had big plans. In two phases, he converted the modest house into the stately renaissance building we know today.

BUILDING PHASE 1 1620–1622
The first stone was laid by Balthasar I's five-year-old godchild and company director-to-be Balthasar II. The old gatehouse and several rooms from Plantin's time made way for a new east wing. The entrance led straight into the first drawing-room, to the right of the chimney.

A type-foundry was added and on the north side a gallery with an upper storey to block out the view of the rental houses. Balthasar I wanted to procure them all. His father had already bought the *Houten Passer*. In 1620 he acquired the *IJzeren Passer* through his aunt Henrietta Plantin. That same year he also bought the *Vosken* (Little Fox). Unfortunately, he missed out on the *Zilveren* and *Koperen Passer*. He had to compensate the owner to build against these buildings.

Balthasar I had the interiors sumptuously decorated with sculpted beams, ornamental staircases and stately fireplaces. The walls of the new drawing-rooms were lined with portraits of his ancestors and friends, painted by his childhood friend Peter Paul Rubens. Together the two also created the beautifully illustrated baroque book.

BUILDING PHASE 2 1637–1640
Balthasar I now turned his attention to the business accommodation. The bookshop moved from Kammenstraat to the main building on the Vrijdagmarkt; to this end he had

Arcade in the inner courtyard, built by Balthasar I Moretus in order to hide the rented houses from view.

The Lion Staircase provides access to the libraries upstairs. It is a fine example of the luxurious joinery with which the family had their house decorated.

BALTHASAR MORETVS

already bought the *Bonte Huid* (Colourful Hide). That building was located rather inconveniently between the office and the wash house, so he split it up. Downstairs on the garden side he created a bookshop and office and upstairs a room and attic. Again godchild Balthasar II, now a young man of twenty-two, laid the first stone.

The other part of the *Bonte Huid* on Hoogstraat was let out. The house and the new shop now had a grand entrance on Hoogstraat. Sculptor Artus Quellinus sculpted the relief with an allegory of the *Gulden Passer*. In 1644 the relief was moved to the entrance on the Vrijdagmarkt, where it still hangs today above the entrance to the museum.

Balthasar I had bookcases built in the new rooms in the west wing above the shop to accommodate his growing library. It was 1691 before they moved to their current location. They are some of the finest in the world.

A floor was added above the printing house and the gallery was extended to just in front of the wash house. The four wings of his mansion now formed a single entity. The Antwerp sculptor Hans van Mildert made busts of Christopher Plantin, Jan I Moretus and Justus Lipsius for the new inner courtyard. Subsequent generations kept up the tradition and added to the row with busts of every director. Today the inner courtyard with this 'wall of fame' is the most beautiful in Antwerp, but even in Balthasar's time the house with its garden was a tourist attraction, visited by kings, princes and other VIPs.

Part of the correctors' room. Although the door in the back wall now leads nowhere, it may once have been an entrance to the *Bonte Huid*, which is located behind it.

PP. 142–143: Portrait busts in the inner courtyard extol the illustrious ancestry of the family.

The new
bookshop (1700).

Subsequent generations

PERIOD 1641–1714

1658 The *IJzeren Passer*, the *Houten Passer* and the *Vosken* were no longer let out, but added to the main house. The *Houten Passer* served as a stable. The stock of books was stored upstairs.

1660 Balthasar II acquired *De Gulden Lelie* (The Golden Lily) on the Vrijdagmarkt. He had a kitchen installed.

1655 Balthasar II created a private chapel. It is not certain if it was already in the big library. It may only have been given its definitive shape in 1757 with the purchase of the painting *Christ on the cross*. The altar under the painting disappeared when the house became a museum.

1714 After the death of Anna Maria de Neuf, widow of Balthasar III, an inventory of the estate is drawn up. The notary's clerk went through the whole house, from the small marble drawing-room (now Room 1), via the gallery to the office with the correctors' bench, the small office, the Lipsius Room, the presses, the wash house and the male employees' room next to the gatehouse. He continued on his way up the stair tower of the gatehouse building and on through the glass office, through a succession of bed-rooms (interrupted by the sorting-room and the correctors' room), the library in three rooms, the last of which housed a billiards table. The aristocratic family set greater store by privacy. The shop moved to the *IJzeren Passer,* so that the sometimes all too inquisitive customers no longer had to go through the inner courtyard to the bookshop. It is still there today.

The altar painting still hangs in its original place in the big library, although the altar itself disappeared after 1876.

The major building campaign

EIGHTEENTH CENTURY

1761-1763 The Moretuses, now one of the richest families in Antwerp, modernized the house and added the grandeur that befitted their status. Over the years they had bought five of the row of seven small houses next to the gatehouse on the Vrijdagmarkt. Now they took the demolition hammer to them and replaced them with the beautiful classical wing designed by the Antwerp architect Engelbert Baets. The new wing in French style housed a spacious entrance hall, a ceremonious stairwell, a kitchen and a dining-room. Theodoor de Bruyn decorated the walls with pastoral scenes. The three drawing-rooms on the inner courtyard were now light rooms with large windows.

1798 The family purchased the house next to the *Vosken* and the *Koperen Passer*.

1803 The Moretuses acquired the last two of the seven small houses on the Vrijdagmarkt.

1819 The family added the *Zilveren Passer* to its property portfolio.

PP. 146–147: Engelbert Baets, *Design for the façade*.

Engelbert Baets, *Design for an eighteenth century drawing room*, which suffered serious damage in 1945. The drawing room was restored in 2006.

What is now the tapestry room used to be a stable. An old photo from 1877 shows the gateways. Nowadays, you can still see the arch where the gateways were situated. The former function of these rooms is also seen in the damaged pillars and the iron balls that served to protect the pillars from the carriages driving past.

From house to museum

On 20 April 1876 Count Edward Moretus sold the main house and all the appertaining buildings to the City of Antwerp, bringing to an end 300 years of family life here. The City carried out the necessary renovation work and a year later the house opened its doors as a museum, heralding the start of 140 years of museum history. The drawing-rooms on the inner courtyard were restored to their sixteenth-century appearance. New passageways improved visitor flow through the complex. The old stable was converted into a museum room, the wash house into a kitchen.

1903 A small house containing exhibition galleries was built next to the wash house. An educational area catered for children and adults.

1936 The Print Room was re-housed in a building on the former site of two small houses on the corner of the Vrijdagmarkt and Heilige Geeststraat.

1940-1945 During the Second World War the collection was transferred to the safety of the Château de Lavaux-Sainte-Anne (to the south of Namur). During the Ardennes Offensive it was hidden in the cellars of the National Bank. On 2 January 1945 a flying bomb destroyed most of the Vrijdagmarkt. Miraculously, it missed the museum but the force of the blast caused severe damage. The corner house did not survive the attack.

These photos, taken on a cold winter's morning in January 1945, give an idea of the damage done to Vrijdagmarkt and the house. Restoration did not begin until several years later.

To specify his fortune, Balthasar II drew up detailed inventories of his possessions in 1658 and in 1662. Besides the company's assets and liabilities, and all the immoveables and valuable art objects, the detailed lists also contained the linen and dinnerware, art cabinets, all the tables (he describes 22 of them), pistols, globes, instruments and gold leather, down to the last chipped chocolate cup. He estimated the total value of the house (40,000 fl), printing house (24,000 fl), personal library and manuscripts (10,000 fl), jewellery (6,039 fl 11 st), gold and silver (6,519 fl 18 st) and miscellaneous items (17,861 fl) at 104,409 fl, 29 st!

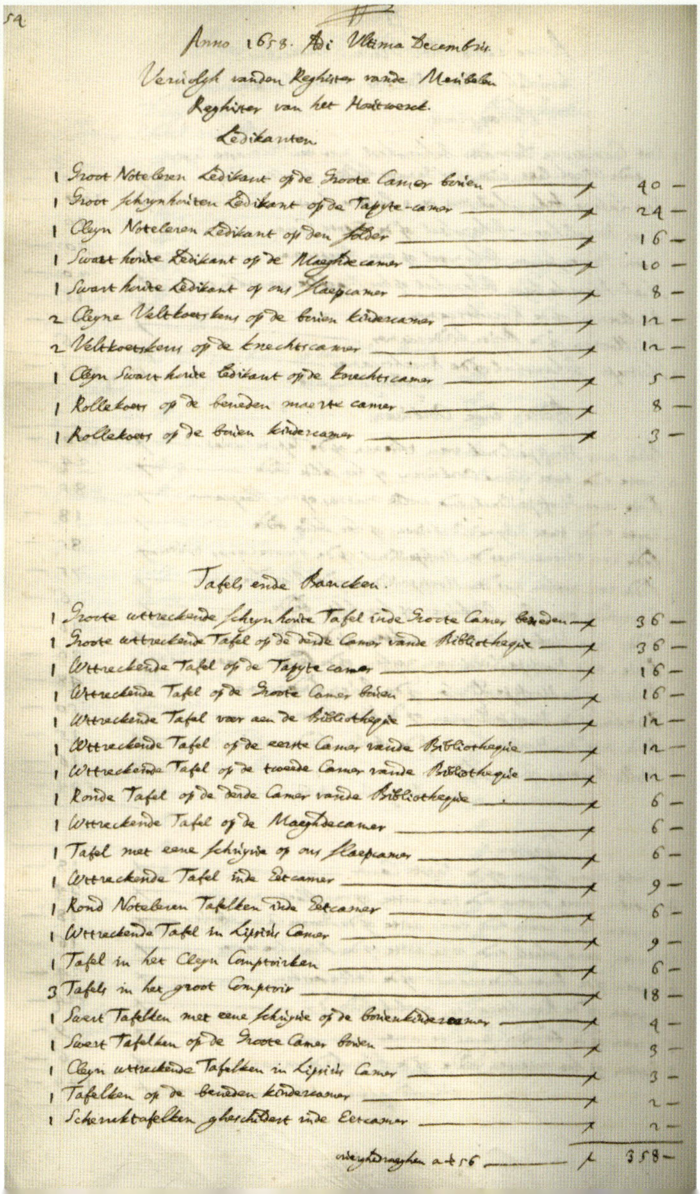

59

Anno 1658. Adi Ultima Decembris.

Vervolgh vanden Register vande Meubelen

Register van het Houtwerck.

Ledikanten

1	Groot Noteleren Ledikant op de Groote Camer boven ƒ	40 –
1	Groot schrynhouten Ledikant op de Tapyte-camer ƒ	24 –
1	Cleyn Noteleren Ledikant op den Solder ƒ	16 –
1	Swart houte Ledikant op de Maeghdecamer ƒ	10 –
1	Swart houte Ledikant op ons Slaepcamer ƒ	8 –
2	Cleyne Veltkoetskens op de boven kindercamer ƒ	12 –
2	Veltkoetskens op de knechtscamer ƒ	12 –
1	Cleyn Swart houte Ledikant op de knechtscamer ƒ	5 –
1	Rollekoets op de beneden meerte camer ƒ	8 –
1	Rollekoets op de boven kindercamer ƒ	3 –

Tafels ende Bancken.

1	Groote uttreckende schrynhoute Tafel inde Groote Camer beneden ƒ	36 –
1	Groote uttreckende Tafel op de derde Camer vande Bibliotheque ƒ	36 –
1	Uttreckende Tafel op de Tapyte camer ƒ	16 –
1	Uttreckende Tafel op de Groote Camer boven ƒ	16 –
1	Uttreckende Tafel voor aen de Bibliotheque ƒ	12 –
1	Uttreckende Tafel op de eerste Camer vande Bibliotheque ƒ	12 –
1	Uttreckende Tafel op de tweede Camer vande Bibliotheque ƒ	12 –
1	Ronde Tafel op de derde Camer vande Bibliotheque ƒ	6 –
1	Uttreckende Tafel op de Maeghdecamer ƒ	6 –
1	Tafel met eene schuyve op ons Slaepcamer ƒ	6 –
1	Uttreckende Tafel inde Eetcamer ƒ	9 –
1	Rond Noteleren Tafelken inde Eetcamer ƒ	6 –
1	Uttreckende Tafel in Lipsius Camer ƒ	9 –
1	Tafel in het Cleyn Comptoirken ƒ	6 –
3	Tafels in het groot Comptoir ƒ	18 –
1	Swert Tafelken met eene schuyve op de bovenkindercamer ƒ	4 –
1	Swert Tafelken op de Groote Camer boven ƒ	3 –
1	Cleyn uttreckende Tafelken in Lipsius Camer ƒ	3 –
1	Tafelken op de beneden kindercamer ƒ	2 –
1	Schenektafelken gheschildert inde Eetcamer ƒ	2 –
	overgedraghen a° 56 ƒ	358 –

1947-1951 After the war, restoration work was essential. The renovated museum reopened its doors in 1951.

1980 A typographical workshop and offices were built on the site of the former corner house on the Vrijdagmarkt. It now houses visitor amenities.

2001 The precious family and company archive was included in the UNESCO Memory of the World Register, a catalogue of the world's most prized documentary and audiovisual heritage.

2005 The whole complex and its contents became UNESCO World Heritage.

2016 noA architecten from Brussels were commissioned to build the extension housing a larger reading room and new store-room for the fragile collection. Artist Benoît van Innis came up with a design for the new façade inspired by the old type cases. So thanks to these additions, the museum is still writing history. Over 140 years after opening it is ready for the twenty-first century.

The new depot, designed by noA architecten, 2016.

Balthasar I Moretus originally ordered this group of statues for the gatehouse on Hoogstraat. His nephew Balthasar II had it transferred to the gatehouse on Vrijdagmarkt in 1644. It represents the company logo, with the Golden Compass and the motto 'Labore et Constantia'. The figures of Hercules and Constantia also appear on the painting commissioned by the same Balthasar I from Erasmus II Quellinus.

Artus Quellinus,
Company logo of the Officina Plantiniana, 1639.

Colophon

Authors
Kris Geysen
Dirk Imhof
Iris Kockelbergh
Kristof Selleslach

Coordination
Griet Claerhout and Odette Peterink

Design and typesetting
Thomas Soete

Translation
Alison Mouthaan-Gwillim
Pond Translations

Proofreading
Griet Claerhout

Production and publishing
Snoeck Publishers

Printed and bound in
the European Union
ISBN 978-94-6161-331-8
D/2016/0012/49

Photographic Credits
Joris Luyten, Noortje Palmers, Ans Brys, Sigrid Spinnox, Stefaan De Wickere, Peter Maes, Guy Hutsebaut, Dina Lavrova, Museum Plantin-Moretus

Acknowledgements
Jeroen De Meester, Nico De Brabander
Philip Heylen, Alderman for Culture, the Economy, Urban and Community Maintenance, Heritage and Places of Worship
Steven Thielemans, Director Culture, Sports, Youth and Education of the City of Antwerp
Lies Buyse, Coordinator Museums and Heritage of the City of Antwerp

www.museumplantinmoretus.be
www.snoeckpublishers.be